DEFENSIVE
SHOOTING FOR
REAL-LIFE
ENCOUNTERS

DEFENSIVE
SHOOTING FOR
REAL-LIFE
ENCOUNTERS

A CRITICAL LOOK AT CURRENT
TRAINING METHODS

Paladin Press
Boulder, Colorado

RALPH MROZ

Also by Ralph Mroz:

Extreme Close-Quarters Shooting: A Critical Analysis of
   Contact-Distance Shooting Tactics (video)
Tactical Defensive Training for Real-Life Encounters: Practical
   Self-Preservation for Law Enforcement

Defensive Shooting for Real-Life Encounters:
A Critical look at Current Training Methods
by Ralph Mroz

Copyright © 2000 by Ralph Mroz

ISBN 13: 978-1-58160-094-X
Printed in the United States of America

Published by Paladin Press, a division of
Paladin Enterprises, Inc.
Gunbarrel Tech Center
7077 Winchester Circle
Boulder, Colorado 80301 USA
+1.303.443.7250

Direct inquiries and/or orders to the above address.

Visit our Web site at www.paladin-press.com

TABLE OF

Contents

Acknowledgments

I do not think in a vacuum. I've benefited from the knowledge of many others who have been gracious enough to teach me and discuss things with me. Among others too numerous to mention, I'm proud to know and am grateful to the following men in particular: Harry Adams, Mas Ayoob, Mike Boyle, Pres Covey, John Farnam, Mark Jacques, Dave Spaulding, Andy Stanford, and Walt Rauch. They don't agree with everything I've written here, but they encourage me to spout and help me refine my thinking.

Steve Wenger, a scientist by training and a noted firearms trainer, spent an uncountable number of hours helping me "get right" the biochemistry and physiology of stress and vision for the chapter on point shooting.

Lou Chiodo, the architect of the California Highway Patrol's (CHP's) firearms program, was generous with his personal time and allowed me to participate in some of the CHP's training. If all trainers cared as much as Lou, the walls would be a lot barer.

Bert DuVernay, the director of the Smith & Wesson Academy, is a correspondent and friend who is unselfish with his time. He is always willing to help me understand a point or to otherwise help me out. Bert is also one of the finest thinkers in this area and contributed the last two chapters in this book.

Finally, thanks to Harry Kane, editor of *Combat Handguns,* for allowing my byline to appear alongside those of his outstanding cadre of real-world writers. It's an honor. Many of these chapters first appeared as columns or articles in *Combat Handguns.* Thanks also to *Guns* magazine, where the extreme close-quarter shooting chapter first appeared as an article (under a pseudonym).

Foreword

I had been reading Ralph's magazine articles for some time before he telephoned me to discuss an article I had written about police patrol rifles in the Smith & Wesson Academy newsletter. Working with Ralph confirmed the impressions I had formed from reading his work. He is quick to critically examine long-held assumptions about training, very methodical in his research, and doesn't take himself overly seriously. That last quality is perhaps the most important to making a lasting contribution to this field.

This is a book that has been needed for some time. It addresses issues of importance to defensive shooters in a scholarly, yet very readable, manner. All too often, books on this subject either approach critical survival issues with shallow research or base conclusions on what happens on the competition field. This book avoids both those traps.

Peace officers, trainers, and armed citizens can all benefit by considering what Ralph has to say. His propositions are practical, straightforward, and well researched. Countless long conversations with Ralph have caused me to reexamine many of my views on both practicing and teaching defensive skills. I'm sure this book will have the same effect on you.

Bert DuVernay
Director, Smith & Wesson Academy
Springfield, Massachusetts
August 1999

CHAPTER 1

Context and Introduction

Any physical discipline, it seems, goes through a series of predictable stages. In the early years, practitioners "just do it." There isn't a great deal of introspection about how it's done or about its various components. One learns by trial and error or by mimicking a skilled practitioner. Eventually the people with the greatest reputation build up a coterie of followers, and a "school of thought" is born. Like religious devotees, the followers of the great practitioners eventually codify "the (one) way it's done." Techniques are defined; deviation is discouraged, and other schools are disparaged. Details of technique are isolated and analyzed.

In all of this "progress" some insight is gained and some advancements are made in the effectiveness of the discipline's practice. However, context is often lost, and the hyper-refinement of detail can lead to endless internecine struggles and emphasis on the irrelevant. The end goal of the discipline is lost and its practice becomes the performance of only "correct" technique.

We've seen this progression in fields as diverse as the social sciences (to take a nonphysical-skills example) and the martial arts (to use a closer-to-home physical skills example). In the social sciences, the original goal of learning how society is put together and operates has degenerated into the academic mental masturbation that is all too familiar to anyone who has spent time in a university environment. The research is so narrow, its assumptions so artificially constrained, its data gathering so flawed, that the results are doomed to either utter irrelevance, complete uselessness, or both. In the martial arts, the goal of winning a violent encounter has been reduced to the practice of artificial kata, gymnastic stunts, and the absence of full-contact sparring from most schools.

The defensive firearms discipline seems to have followed this same progression. In the "old days," gunslingers simply did what worked for them, relying on instinct and whatever wisdom they could glean from the men who proceeded them. After World War II, however, the trend toward isolation, analysis, and codification began in earnest in this most personal and vital of areas. Much good came of this, and a good many lives were undoubtedly saved by the insights of those involved. But while progress was made, true progress was soon arrested as the scene became politicized and the stultification set in. "Gurus" laid down their gospels and the discipline made most of its progress in the only semirelated area of sporting competition.

We are much better off today than we were in 1950, but we've plateaued. It's time to move on. This book is about where we are, what is right about this state, and what we need to do to resume progress. It is about goals and mind-set as much as training regimens. This book is also about correcting some quirks that have managed to either hang on in current training or insinuate themselves into it.

The overriding theme of the book is that we must face reality. We must start first from what really happens in a deadly force encounter and then design our defensive system—training, weapon, and carry—to match it. We must train as reality dictates, not as the constraints of our range or the whims of convenience dictate.

Quite properly, the question arises, "Who are you to write such a book?" From one perspective, I am nobody. Fortunately, I have yet to return hostile gunfire—and if I had, I doubt that I would feel the need to talk or write much about the experience. Neither am I a member or alumnus of a prestigious SpecOps community. I have not won any significant competitions, and indeed, my shooting skills sometimes dip rather lower than I feel comfortable with. My experience and skills are therefore limited. I write this book as a researcher and thinker, and its merit depends on the facts that I cite and the logic by which I draw conclusions. To be sure, these are the legs upon which any treatise of this sort must stand, since the experience of even the most decorated person is limited—and is further limited by circumstances to less-than-universal validity. I must trust that this book will be judged by these criteria.

CHAPTER 2

Training as if Reality Were Real

You Still Have to Sweat

I was talking with a friend a while ago, and he took me to task for harping on the necessity of empty-hand skills, even for people carrying firearms. "You can't expect everyone to be a macho superman," he admonished. Well, I'm sure he has long forgotten his passing comment, but it sure monopolized my brain for a few days.

WHAT SHOULD WE EXPECT FROM PEOPLE?

First, I guess, is the notion of expectations. In the larger sense, I don't expect anyone to do anything except stay out of my way, good libertarian that I am. Have a nice life and all that. But in a narrower sense, if someone professes to be a student of a discipline, it *is* disappointing when he refuses to face squarely up to the issues involved. Take the discipline of self-protection, which is what we're talking about here. Most folks seem to go about it all wrong. Mistakenly, they first study one of its subdisciplines—martial arts, guns, or what have you. Then they view the real-life problems of self-protection through the lens of their particular subdiscipline. Martial arts people see self-protection as a series of martial arts problems, largely ignoring, for example, the issues of multiple and/or armed assailants. Gun people see self-protection as a set of shooting scenarios, always assuming that they'll be able to get the gun in their hand and generally ignoring the issues of less-than-lethal force or encounters too close in to allow access to their gun.

Naturally, this approach is backward. The logical and tactically sound thing to do is to first analyze a problem and then choose the tactics you need to solve it. That is, first understand the dynamics of a violent encounter, and then choose the appropriate tactics to master.

LEARN FROM MY MISTAKES

I started out in the martial arts decades ago, and for years was as guilty of this same backassward attitude as anyone. I hated guns (no, I'm not joking). In my mind they were for fat, lazy rednecks without the ambition or self-discipline to sweat in the dojo! Then one day, about 10 years into the arts, I had an honest conversation with myself:

"OK, you've got 10 years of training. You get into a fight with someone without much training or experience. What are your odds?"

"Good."

"Right. Now this guy has training and/or experience. What're your odds now?"

"50/50?"

"Close enough. Now there's two guys, both without training, but mean. Odds?"

"I dunno, probably less than 50/50, in all honesty."

"Right. Now two guys with training."

"My odds suck."

"One guy with a knife?"

"Oh shit!"

The conversation went on for a few more steps, but you get the idea.

The next week I was looking for a pistol, and after I had acquired basic marksmanship skills, I made the pilgrimage to several national schools. The lesson here is one of overcoming prejudice and viewing the discipline of self-protection realistically. You need skills, you get 'em. Should be simple.

Most assaults occur at very close distances, and there's often no time to draw a gun.

THE LEAD-COLORED LENS

Now, getting back to my friend's complaint, my "expectations" (in the sense described above) fall short when I witness the myopia—the lead-colored lens, so to speak—through which many people who carry a gun for self-protection view that discipline. The fact is that most street violence occurs at very close distances—close enough for your assailant to touch you, or at least to hit or stab you with a single step. Simple physiology folks: there is no way you can draw a gun from concealment at that distance before your attacker is all over you. Your gun, by itself, is useless under these conditions (just as my empty-hands skills by themselves were useless in many street situations)! Without the empty-hand skills to create the time and/or distance to draw your

On the range, 5 yards is considered "close in." In reality, most deadly assaults occur at much closer range.

weapon, you might as well have not bothered to study the gun at all. While this is certainly a good argument for going about in a continuous state of condition yellow, *please*—we're intelligent adults here—don't anyone write in to say that heightened awareness will save you in all of these situations. Sometimes s*** just happens.

What's happening here is that gun people are falling into the same trap that I did, only in reverse. When all self-defense problems are viewed as shooting problems, then you practice a lot of shooting at distances that keep the shooting interesting and challenging. On the range, 5 yards is considered "close-in shooting;" on the street, 5 yards is almost in the next time zone. Sure, if trouble manifests itself on the street at 5 yards, then you will kick into condition orange or red, and you probably will have time to get to your weapon. But it usually won't. On the range, drawing and shooting is hardly ever done within touching distance of the target; on the street, that's where it all happens. What little practice is done at touching range tends to be either the flawed "step-back" technique or the highly specialized speed-rock, which is not applicable in most situations. To a person for whom self-protection means only shooting, the logically and empirically evident necessity of complementary empty-hand skills is simply blanked out. This is illogical, self-deluding, and just plain stupid.

YOU GOTTA SWEAT

Part of the reason for this self-deception may be that a practical level empty-hands skill is often more difficult to obtain than a similar level of shooting skill. Realistic empty-hand skill comes from sweating and from getting hit. This hurts. Practical self-protection skill comes from developing a fighting spirit, which is often more difficult—and for many people, much more uncomfortable—to develop than a "sport attitude." This may be the reason (at least in my limited expe-rience) that martial artists often make the transition to prac-tical skills with the gun more easily than gun people realize the same integration.

So should I expect people to be competent in both empty-hand skills and firearms? I guess I don't see much choice if we're discussing self-protection. That's simply what it takes. Whether it's easy or not . . . well, that's a different ques-tion—one that goes back to my original bias. Are guns really for fat, lazy rednecks without the ambition or self-discipline to sweat in the dojo?

CHAPTER 3

The Range Effect
A Deadly Syndrome

The range is flat, open, unobstructed, well lit, safe, unidirectional, stress-free, and clear of distractions. The street, or wherever else you'll have to fight for your life, is not.

Range targets are flat, static, facing head-on, quiet, nonpersonal, and nonthreatening. The person trying to kill you isn't.

So obviously, range training, no matter how "practical" or "tactical" is not real-world training. This is not a hypothesis or an opinion. It is a plain fact. You can shoot high-speed, low-drag drills all day against paper (or steel) targets and not touch the reality of a genuine encounter.

THREE STAGES

We are stuck in the second of three stages of gun skills development. These three stages are as follows.

The author shoots under the supervision of Blackwater Lodge and Training Center Chief Instructor Al Clark. Blackwater and all the other good schools have extensive range facilities where you learn to shoot, but they also have facilities for realistic force-on-force training where you learn to fight.

Stage 1: Grounding in the Basics

Beginning fundamentals need to be developed at this first stage. Safety, basic gun handling, marksmanship, trigger control, sight alignment, etc. (No matter how advanced we are, we can all use occasional brushing up on these most basic of skills.)

Sight alignment, grip, and trigger control are the basics in which you must acquire a grounding in Stage 1 training.

Stage 2 drills include shooting from cover, shooting weak-handed, shooting while moving, and so on. They are still just "swimming on dry land."

Stage 2: Range Drills—Simple to Complex

From beginner-level bull's-eye shooting in Stage 1, it's common and prudent to move on to progressively more difficult range drills. Drills might include shooting from cover, while kneeling, while prone, weak-handed, while moving, or one-handed. It's here that shooting for speed as well as accuracy is introduced, as is shooting at multiple targets, decision targets, and so on. Most of the training today—at police academies and even at national-level schools—stops at this level. But while static shooting at targets can get ingeniously complex and difficult—look at any IPSC (International Practical Shooting Confederation) match—it's still just shooting at paper.

Force-on-force drills (Stage 3) are where you learn how to actually defend yourself under real-life assault conditions.

Stage 3: Force-on-Force Scenarios

The goal of this next level of training, the place that we logically ought to be aiming for, is to replicate as closely as possible the fights we'll be in. This kind of training requires the use of real guns (or something very similar) modified to fire nonlethal projectiles. Here we're talking about targets that think, move, and shoot back! (Admittedly, even in a simulated force-on-force exercise, we don't duplicate the level of stress you get in a real fight—after all, we know we're not going to get killed. But it's the closest thing we have available now.)

Stage 1 is where we all start. Stage 2 is where we develop useful skills and instinctive motor movements under stress. Stage 3 is where we learn to actually fight.

Each stage has a point of diminishing returns. No one would argue that refining marksmanship, or breath control, or trigger control in Stage 1 past a certain point is meaningless in terms of practical survival skills. What we seem to have forgotten is that there's a point of diminishing returns in Stage 2, too. Shortening a little time between A-Zone doubles[1], or shaving small fractions of a second off a reload, or working on minute decreases in draw time, is irrelevant past a certain point. Once we've reached that point, it's time to move on to Stage 3 training. But today, few trainers and students move beyond this static-target, intermediate stage of training. Indeed, many trainers today seem to actively promote their students' retardation by indefinitely perpetuating the stay at Stage 2.

FEEDING THE MARKS

Why? There are cynical and noncynical reasons. Certainly few students are really ready for force-on-force encounters. Their skills just aren't there yet, or they don't possess the other attributes necessary in a fight: fitness, strength, speed (of body movement), empty-hand skills (most real encounters occur within touching distance), and just plain fighting spirit. Also, this is the stage where the gamesmen live (some, such as IPSC master-class competitors, at awesomely high levels), and many shooters are primarily interested—whether they admit it or not—in playing games. For most people, games are much more comfortable and much more fun than replicating a real-life encounter. That's fine, but we shouldn't confuse skill at games with fighting skill.

From a cynical point of view, trainers have a vested interest in keeping their paying customers at Stage 2. By making the drills here ever more complex, and by making arbitrary standards increasingly difficult—way past the point of any likely practical necessity—they ensure a continued supply of students striving to meet these goals. If they then add the lure of their own self-anointed badge of mastership—usually some title including the words "Combat" and "Master"—then the student is even more driven to accomplish these artificial and arbitrary objectives—and to keep on paying to learn at the master's feet. This is an old con—I've seen it for the last 25 years in the martial arts. Most martial arts schools keep their students busy by endlessly practicing street-useless katas and ineffective "advanced techniques." They grant their badge of mastership—the black belt—to people who've never punched much more than empty air. Very few do full-contact/full-speed sparring. This is, after all, just good business; realistic training doesn't make the instructor look as perfect as empty-air drills and scares the marks—I mean the students—away.

Do I wish I could break multiple bricks with my bare hands or score a 10-yard A-Zone double tap in one second from the holster? Sure. But I'd much rather have spent the training time necessary to accomplish those goals in the ring getting hit and developing a reliable left hook or in a "funhouse" learning how to shoot thinking opponents before they "kill" me.

Are all trainers really this deceitful? No, but it *is* in their best interest to perpetuate—perhaps indefinitely—their students' stay at Stage 2. Not the least of the reasons is that so long as they can reliably outperform their students on Stage 2 artificial drills, they continue to look good and attract more students. By contrast, anyone who's ever participated in a force-on-force exercise knows that sometimes, no matter how good you are, you lose. Real life is harsh and is mostly a matter of probabilities. I *know* that I can shave two-tenths of a second off my draw and fire time if I practice hard enough, but the only result I can be sure of if I pursue force-on-force training is that I'll lose somewhat less often.

Shooting at hostage/bad-guy targets is a widespread, amusing, and totally dangerous practice. If you think you can make this shot in the heat of combat while all parties are moving and screaming, you are probably mistaken. It's foolish to train your reflexes to try it.

THE RANGE EFFECT

All of this results in what I call the range effect. That is, the creeping prevalence of artificial behaviors and skills into Stage 2 training. This is exactly what happened to the old Budo martial arts in Japan. These were genuine interpersonal combat disciplines, with their training dictated by the realities of constant war. When peace came to Japan, these practical disciplines devolved into the "arts" we see today on every street corner, each as different as one sort of art can be from another, but all alike in their lack of realism.

We see the range effect in operation whenever a teacher insists that the proper way to execute a 180-degree turn is to pirouette on a toe, or when he or she explains in excruciating detail the exact way to perform a simple side-step. We see it when we are told that the "right" way to shoot is to isolate our upper bodies so as to eliminate any extraneous movement, and thus get the sights on target faster. (While that's true, and while I do get accurate shots off faster that way, if someone is trying to kill me, you can bet that my behind will be in motion!) We see the range effect in an emphasis on stepping-back techniques as a response to close-in threats. (See Chapter 10, "Extreme Close-Quarter Shooting," for the numerous fatal flaws in this technique.) We see it brought to ridiculous heights by subjecting Stage 2 students to hostage targets in front of "shoot" targets. And so on, and so on. (If you think you can really shoot a moving bad guy taking cover behind a moving hostage while you're moving, then try out for your local SWAT team as a designated entry marksman. It's irresponsible to even suggest this to anyone else! Hostage/bad-guy targets, which are perversely so much a mainstay of Stage 2 training, have no place in the responsible training of most people.)

The range effect, the game mentality of too many shooters, the self-interest of trainers, and the humbling difficulty of truly realistic training all combine to make Stage 2 training self-perpetuating. But there's a faint trend developing in the right direction. We are starting to see some trainers move to force-on-force training. This will truly be the area to watch, explore, and research in the next few years. Let's just hope they don't invent some sort of competitive league—complete with a rule book and a board of directors—for it.

1. The A-Zone is the center scoring area on a target, usually a standard IPSC target. Doubles refers to the act of firing two rapid shots into the same area.

CHAPTER 4

Five Deadly Training Traps

Not all, but too many, trainers have their own way of doing things—their "doctrine." In their minds, that "one right way" is the way you do it, damn it, and anyone who tells you differently is a moron, a cheat, or a fraud!

This bad attitude proliferates because the field of firearms training is fraught with three destructive factors: ego, testosterone, and money.

Ego. Firearms handling is a skill held in awe by the general public (even though it's actually less difficult than countless more complex activities). This cultural phenomenon naturally tends to feed the egos of instructors for whom gun skills are the sole form of self-identification.

Testosterone. Culturally, weapons training is regarded as a macho, manly field, and therefore attracts far too many people afflicted with "testosterone poisoning."

Money. Instructors compete, if not directly with each other, then indirectly for the time and money that agencies and individuals have to spend on firearms training.

These three destructive factors have led to a few rounds of doctrinal battles over the last couple decades. Semiautomatic vs. revolver, isosceles vs. Weaver, and 9mm vs. .45 caliber articles have sold a lot of magazines. Now, these were interesting and informative debates, and we learned a lot from them—even if often what we learned was that it really doesn't matter!

Today, these same three factors are generating a new set of doctrinal battles. Believing the wrong side—or in some cases, believing that there is a "right" side—can lead to dysfunctional or even dangerous training. There are also several issues that haven't been discussed enough. Lumping them together, let's take a look.

TRAINING TRAPS

Six Bullets Are Enough

One of the things that seems to be a dead issue now is the old battle between the six-gun and the self-loader for the title of "best gun." These days we all realize that the semiautomatic pistol has significant tactical advantages for most shooters: greater ease of use, speed, accuracy, and firepower. The "automatic" has overcome the only real criticism that was ever leveled at it: unreliability. Although revolvers will always be inherently more reliable, self-loaders from all the major manufacturers are all pretty good these days, particularly with a modicum of maintenance.

On the other hand, we also realize that the revolver is not the crusty anachronism that many believe it to be. A good revolver is a fine defensive weapon, limited only in its abili-

A good revolver is a fine weapon, limited only in its ammunition capacity. It's hardly the mark of an ignorant shooter.

ty to hold just six rounds. In fact, many instructors argue that that's more than enough: "If you need more than six rounds, you've got a shooting problem, not a capacity problem"; "If you can't do it in six, you can't do it in 18"; "The average defender in a gunfight fires 2.3 rounds (or 3.2 rounds, or whatever it is), so what do you need more than six rounds for?"; and "Spray and pray is not a valid alternative to hitting your target" are some of the homey sayings that are offered in support of this position. While I agree with the last one, the rest are, to be polite, just blustering. There are, in fact, very good reasons for choosing as high a capacity pistol as you can comfortably manage.

If your defensive nightmare is average—that is, less than 5 feet and a couple of shots—then sure, any old gun will do, even a derringer. You probably don't even need to aim. However, if it's not average, if there are multiple assailants (which is the trend), if any of them are moving, if any of them are partially behind cover, or if you have to lay down covering fire for another innocent or to effect a retreat, then, by God, you'll thank Providence for each and every round in your "wonder nine."

This is very simple to demonstrate. Get yourself off the range and into a parking lot or shoot-house, issue Simunitions FX marking cartridges (or something like them) to all participants, and run through a truly realistic scenario. You'll then see the truth in this homey aphorism: "You can never be too thin, too rich, or have too much ammunition."

Fire Two, Lower to Ready, Assess, Place Head Shot If Necessary

There are several well-known instructors for whom I have enormous respect who advocate this tactic when under assault. I'm hardly qualified to say that they're wrong, and that's not my intent here, as evidenced by my also taking issue with the alternate technique of firing until they drop from your sights. What I do want to point out is that simple logic alone will tell you that neither tactic is a universal solution—life is more complicated than that, and our training should reflect this reality.

Shooting center of mass until they drop doesn't work if the bad guys are wearing body armor, or when they're so high that they can soak up lots of rounds. There have been too many cases in which the perps soaked up round after round (even of .45s) for this not to be a concern. Note that body armor is perfectly legal to buy, and is widely available.

Firing two, lowering your gun, assessing the situation, and taking a possible head shot is equally problematic. This tactic presumes that if two center-mass rounds don't stop Mr. Bad Guy, then more won't either. And how, exactly, do we know this? How do we know that he won't be stopped by the third, fourth, or fifth round? After all, handgun rounds are horribly underpowered relative to the task at hand. I would like to see a statistically valid, variable-normalized study on this before betting my life on this tactic as a universal cure-all (or "stop-all"). Since most defensive shootings occur at very close distances (closer than 5 feet according to the stats), stopping to evaluate the situation will cost you precious time you really don't have. Further, trying to make a head shot on a moving assailant while you're likely moving and in body-alarm reaction is all but impossible. It's hard enough on static paper targets, on which this tactic is universally demonstrated.

So what's the answer? Well, it's surely not to pretend that real life is amenable to one-tactic-fits-all solutions. If facing up to the complexity and difficulty and sometimes just plain shitty luck of real-life deadly force encounters means that we have to achieve a higher skill level in order to be prepared, then so be it. If we have to stop telling students that an $800 three-day, "advanced" handgun course will prepare them for the street, then that's what we have to do. We need to train in both of these tactics, and more—much, much, more. We need to train with handguns, knives, sticks, and empty hands. With guns, we need to train when and where to fire our rounds with instantaneous decision-making capability. These skills don't come from static range work. You can drill El Presidente[1] all day long and not come close to the reality of the street. You can only prepare for real-life encounters by engaging in simulated real-life role-playing exercises.

Range Exercise Prepares You for the Street

Simple logic will tell you that range training is not training for the street—that the master of the range isn't necessarily the master of a real-life deadly force situation. The logic is unassailable: we can only prepare to face moving,

Gene Zinc of H&K's International Training Division directs a class in MP5 operation. Eventually you move onto force-on-force simulations to become really proficient with this or any weapon.

thinking, attacking human beings in the stairwell of a cramped, crowded, noisy apartment by doing just that. Range training is merely "swimming on dry land." Sooner or later, you have to jump in the water.

I'm sometimes asked how one can tell a realistic martial arts school from one that isn't. I tell them it's simple: look for the FIST suits hanging on the wall. These suits are the only gear on the market that allows reasonably unrestricted motion while allowing the wearer to withstand full-power blows. Hence: no FIST suits, no realistic practice. Likewise with firearms: no Simunitions (or equivalent), no realism.

Why then do totally unrealistic range exercises continue to dominate training, even at many big-name schools? Four reasons:

- the unrealistic ranges are traditional;
- realistic force-on-force ranges are difficult to set up effectively and safely;
- realistic ranges are considered expensive to set up (But really, compared to what—we're talking a few Simunitions or paintball guns and an old building);
- and the reason that covers most of the sins here—realistic man-on-man training can be embarrassing for the instructor. (He is much more likely to lose a real-life encounter than miss a target. It's hard for an instructor to maintain his God-like aura when the students are "killing" him with simulated rounds.)

You Don't Need to Use Your Sights

Actually, the whole matter is complicated, and there's another chapter in this book devoted to it. The bottom line, however, and one on which the late Col. Rex Applegate quite agreed, is that the only hope of hitting targets past very close distances is to use the sights. And so we must become proficient with them. Advocating point shooting as a universal solution, rather than a specific technique for certain circumstances, is downright deceitful.

The Gun Relieves You of Having to Learn Empty-Hand Skills

Since most assaults come from within 5 feet, simple logic will tell you that there's no way you can possibly draw your gun in time to deal with them if you're taken by surprise. You simply cannot see all attacks coming, even in perpetual condition yellow. Ain't gonna happen. Life sucks.

If you are to get to your gun at all, you'll first have to deal with the attack with your empty hands, and even then you still may not create the time or distance to get to your weapon. You'll wind up dealing with most deadly-force attacks empty-handed—whether partially or fully.

When the attack is up close, there's simply no time to draw. You will need empty-hand skills then, no matter how well armed.

Now, it's much harder to get to an acceptable survival level with empty hands than it is with firearms (and I have the broken bones to prove it), and we all know how hard it is to learn to shoot well. Learning empty-hand skills means you'll hurt, you'll have to be in shape, and you'll need discipline. You'll actually sweat!

Why don't our range drills incorporate these necessary empty-hand skills? Frankly, it's because most firearms instructors don't know them and delude themselves about their necessity. Most range instructors seldom drill at less than a few yards, calling *that* "close-quarters shooting." Neither have most range instructors spent any time analyzing the few imperfect techniques taught for belly-to-belly situations. It's much easier to teach marksmanship than it is to teach the spectrum of skills you need to really fight.

In reality, if most deadly attacks occur within 5 feet, shouldn't we spend much of our valuable range time on the combination of empty-hand and firearms skills needed to survive those encounters?

Now, I don't mean to imply that I'm some sort of master of realistic fighting skills. My own range skills are just average (and sometimes worse). Like most people I don't practice enough, and I'm just beginning to incorporate realistic role-playing force-on-force into my training.

What I am saying, though, is that simple logic—applied to street survival—dictates that we spend less time on stagnant range exercises and more time on realistic role-playing drills.

---

1. A standard shooting competition drill. The shooter begins with his back to three targets. On a signal, he turns and fires two rounds into each target, reloads, and fires two more into each.

CHAPTER 5

KIASAP

Keep It as Simple as Possible

I have watched with interest and some amusement the debate over the KISS (Keep It Simple, Stupid) operating principle. Some dislike it, rightly pointing out that what we need to do to survive isn't simple and we aren't stupid. Others embrace it, pointing out—again rightly—that we all get stupid under stress. Both positions are, of course, right.

FIGHTING NATURE

One truth is that there are things that our bodies are hard-wired to do under life-threatening stress. The list of these should be well known by now: tunnel vision, auditory exclusion, distorted sense of time, loss of fine motor control, threat focus, crouching, etc. Trying to fight these reactions is most likely a losing game.

Another truth is that the execution of effective fighting techniques—whether empty-handed or with a firearm—is not hard wired. These techniques are, in fact, very difficult to train. For example, the bullet must generally hit our aggressor within an 8-inch vital area in the center of the chest in order to have a high probability of stopping him. Contrary to popular opinion, it is possible to miss an 8-inch circle at 5 yards (and we won't even talk about head shots). Likewise, if we don't have good trigger control, we'll miss; if the barrel isn't aligned with the target, we'll also miss.

The overriding truth is that there are some reactions we have in life-threatening circumstances that simply can't be fought, while at the same time there are some fighting skills that we absolutely must develop in order to survive, regardless of how hard they are to make instinctive.

Naturally, this scale is a continuous one, with few black and white areas (impossible-to-perform tasks and totally necessary skills), and much gray area in between (skills that can be developed in a greater or smaller amount of time). The job of a competent trainer is to understand which skills lie where along this axis, and to skew his training along this scale according to his audience. Trainers that have "one right way" to do something aren't really teachers but merely opinion holders. And you know what they say about opinions.

KIASAP

The operating principle I choose to embrace is KIASAP— Keep It as Simple as Possible. Do what you gotta do, but don't fight Mother Nature. Some examples of the choices I've made follow. They suit my average ability. You can make your own choices depending on where you are in terms of your own skill development and ease of learning.

The tactical reload is a technique designed to keep instructors in business—not to save your life.

The Tactical Reload

Yes, you want to avoid leaving ammo hanging around collecting dust. But it seems to me that if I'm reloading, then there's nothing more important at that moment than getting my gun restocked with things that go bang. If I really have time for a tactical reload—the "lull" in the action that this technique is taught for—then I'll have time to pick up the ejected magazine and stick it in my pocket. And I'll have a loaded gun in my hand while I'm doing it. Keeping my reloading drills to speed reloads simplifies my training—and doesn't burn up hours mastering a skill I can't see the logic in anyway. Besides, tactical reloads are quite difficult to get the hang of with any smoothness, which brings me to:

The 5-Minute Test

So many techniques, so little time! I simply apply my 5-minute test to determine where I'll spend my precious training time. That is, I give a new technique a try, and if it doesn't seem like a good idea, or I don't get the general hang of it within 5 minutes, I chuck it. Arrogant? Lazy? No, just realistic for me. Experience has shown me that for a shooter of my ability (average) and coordination (a little above average), any technique I'll eventually develop skill in under stress is one that works well for me right off the bat. Basically, trust yourself. If it feels cumbersome and/or stupid, then you're unlikely to get so good at it that it becomes flawless under attack. For example—tactical reloads. None of the ones I've

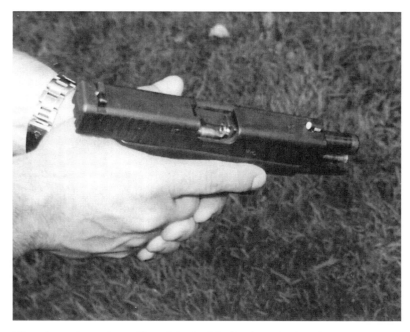

There's no harm in calling this double feed a "double feed." Insisting on calling it a "type such-and-such failure" only makes the instructor look smarter than he or she is.

been shown ever felt comfortable to me, so when forced to do them, I do them the way I instinctively always have: I rip the old one out of the gun and stick it in my belt in front of the belly button, acquire and insert a new one, and do whatever seems appropriate with the old one at that point.

Nomenclature

Shooting a gun effectively is hard enough already. We shouldn't deliberately make it harder than we need to by obfuscating its concepts with unnecessary jargon. Calling a failure to go into battery a "Type 1 malfunction" (or whatever it's called) instead of a "failure to go into battery" does nothing to make it easier for me to learn to recognize the problem or to clear it. Likewise with calling a stovepipe a "Type X" failure, and so on. Also, if I'm carrying my pistol "cocked and locked," all I do is artificially inflate the perception of my own expertise by insisting on calling this state "Condition 1," or calling the "chamber loaded, hammer down" state "Condition 2," and so on. Plain language makes it easier for students to learn, while confusing language serves only to make it all seem mysterious and make the teacher appear omnipotent.

Movement

Not to blow my own horn, but sometimes I just go off and start walking without even thinking about what my legs are doing! I can do this highly skilled task because I'm a trained professional—don't try it at home, kids.

Actually, I've been taking steps since I was 1 year old. I think the skill is pretty well ingrained by now. Do I really need to worry about unweighting one leg, moving it just so far in a particular direction, and setting it down with X percent of my weight on it when I need to move and fire? Obviously, no. So why do some instructors insist on wasting our time "teaching" this stuff to us? I'll not comment on that now, but this is the sort of thing to which we can easily apply the KIASAP principle without stretching our brains too far. Do what's come naturally all your life.

Stance

When I started shooting after a decade in the martial arts, I found that the "Chapman" (or modified Weaver) stance came naturally to me. I shot that way for some time and while going through a couple schools. But when I shot my first bowling pin match—surprise—I instinctively shot from an isosceles stance! Even IPSC shooters, once the last bastion of Weaver shooters, seem to have mostly gone to the isosceles these days. This confirms what countless teachers and observers have related: that no matter how they're trained, most people revert to isosceles shooting when they're in combat (or just under the stress of a local competition). This fact, as well as a couple decades of testing, has validated the isosceles stance as the preferred way to teach shooting to most people. But I notice something else now, years after that first pin match. The stance I instinctively assume now varies with the situation. During the close-in environment of house clearings, a Weaver position is sometimes instinctive. During other types of shooting, I sometimes find myself in a Chapman stance, and sometimes in an isosceles. I've come to not care about it anymore, figuring that my body is automatically doing what it can to give me the best advantage in the circumstances and physical position I'm in.

CONCLUSION

Every time you train, you are making a choice about what you are training into yourself. If your goal is practical defense, then try to make your choices by recognizing the distinction between things that you must master and things that you aren't likely to. In other words, KIASAP.

CHAPTER 6

The Limits of Practical Match Training

I recently spent a pleasant day observing a national-level International Defensive Pistol Association (IDPA) match. What I saw was a lot of people having a lot of fun in a friendly atmosphere. But I left the match with some musings regarding practical training and contests.

The IDPA was formed as a sort of reaction to the direction in which IPSC had gone. There's no question that IPSC has really become a game of fast-and-fancy shooting, without much relationship to real-life practical tactics. (While this is by and large true, see my caveats on dismissing IPSC altogether below.) There's nothing wrong with IPSC's direction, of course, and there's much right with a sport that brings flash, money, and participants into shooting. But the *practical* had gone out of IPSC, and the IDPA was designed to fill the void. Courses of fire in IDPA matches are designed to resemble real situations, and the hardware allowed is severely restricted by class in order to be street-realistic. Score is based on time and accuracy and restrictions such as dictating a tactical reload rather than a speed reload. Penalties are assessed for errors such as leaning too far around cover rather than pieing it out.[1]

A master-class IPSC shooter was the chief course designer for this IDPA match, and his IPSC background served him well. Familiar with all of the gamesmanship tricks in shooting matches, he was able to wring out much of the potential for them in the courses he designed. As I was listening to him tell me about this wringing-out process, I had my first insight into how the gamesmen in the shooting sports must approach their craft. Now, I have nothing whatsoever against the gamesmen or their games (and I'm not using the term disparagingly—just descriptively). Indeed, I admire and even covet their skill greatly. But, in a blinding flash of the obvious, it occurred to me that these are people who approach shooting—that is, the firing of real bullets out of a real gun— as a game! To them, a shooting match is essentially an advanced game of pinball. I realized at that moment just how wide the gulf in psychologies is between the people who shoot guns as a sport (the gamesmen) and those who shoot strictly for defensive purposes (the martial artists).

No matter how hard I try, I just cannot bring myself to view the pistol on my hip as a flipper and the rounds in my magazine as pinballs. Every time I think of my gun, I cannot help but think of the serious duty it is there for, and the immense responsibility I have undertaken by carrying it. My pistol represents my life and the lives of my loved ones to me. It is simply never thought of as a toy.

I'm not implying that many gamesmen don't regard (at least some of) their guns as defensive tools, too, nor am I remotely implying that gamesmen are unsafe or casual about the dangerous nature of their toys. I'm only pointing out that their guns are, at least much of the time, toys to them, and that this consideration is simply not possible for a martial artist. And anytime you have a match with scores, you can't avoid some degree of gamesmanship.

Which brings us to the limits of realistic training in a match format. While far more realistic than most IPSC stages, and through no fault of the course designers, the IDPA stages I saw did not completely reflect reality. I will admit that I've read descriptions of other IDPA matches that involved a radio-controlled paintball gun firing at the participants, which is a big step toward simulated reality. Nonetheless, I suspect that you cannot eliminate all the

The wrong way to shoot from a stationary car. Yet this is what one national-class IDPA match required.

One right way to handle the same situation. Perhaps a better way would be to bail out onto the ground and get behind the vehicle—but you can't do that safely at a match.

gamesmanship from any objectively scored and safe match. Doing so—requiring that all participants act with utmost tactical soundness at all times—would probably require an unacceptably subjective scoring system and would not be possible on most ranges.

For example, at the match I attended, one stage required the shooter to exit a car, engage targets on the exited side of the vehicle, move around the back of the vehicle, and engage targets on the opposite side of it. Every participant that I saw engaged the targets on the exited side of the vehicle by kneeling or squatting in front of the opened car door and shooting out the opened window. They then ran around the car and engaged the targets on the opposite side from the rear of the vehicle, shot to slide-lock, performed a speed reload, and continued to engage these targets until the end of the exercise.

Whether these tactics were demanded by the stage rules or simply chosen by the competitors to minimize time, they were not tactically sound. To wit: using a car door for cover, exposing much of themselves through the window opening, and not reloading when they got behind the vehicle. Also, most competitors performed their (speed) reload while their pistol and much of their shooting arm and shoulder remained out from cover. A purely tactical scenario would have demanded that the competitors use hard cover—probably by bailing out onto the ground, getting to the rear of the vehicle as fast as possible, and shooting from there—and penalized them for not reloading behind cover prior to changing engagement sides, and deducted points for exposing themselves during a reload. However, these demands would probably also have made the stage too athletically demanding for many competitors, resulted in loaded guns being pointed uprange at times, and required subjective judgments about competitor exposure.

On another stage, competitors had to open a door and engage a moving target from the doorway prior to entering

Entering a doorway like this is a good way to get killed—yet it, too, was required at a local IDPA match.

Everyone knows (or damn well should know) that the right way to enter a doorway is to pie it out—but in a match where time counts, this realistic and safe technique is at odds with winning.

the "room." Clearly, completely realistic tactics would have demanded that the shooter enter the room as fast as possible to escape the fatal funnel[2] and drive to one of the room's corners while doing so. However, these tactically sound movements would also cause the shooter's gun to be pointed in many unsafe directions on the range.

How can we judge tactical soundness, in any case? Who is to say that you did or did not expose too much of yourself from cover, and on what basis can someone who is not downrange judge this? As it was, the match director had a devil of a time designing courses so that the judges could determine whether the shooter was really slicing the pie around cover or just "hanging out" from it. How do we safely simulate the 360-degree x 360-degree nature of real-world problems on a flat 180-degree range?

In law enforcement agencies that do scenario-based training, judging a student's tactical performance is usually done through one-on-one critiques from the instructor, which is a pretty subjective activity and not one that works in a match setting where each shooter must get a score. Of course, we could devise training events in which our performance in solving tactical problems was judged by a panel of experts, but these would be training events with subjective feedback, not matches with quantitative scores.

Competitions are, by their very nature, games. Anytime you have a clock ticking, participants will bend any tactically sound rules to gain an advantage. Not only does this destroy the proper tactical mind-set, it develops unsound tactical habits. Either we can perform paper-target drills with survival as our primary objective and be judged subjectively, or we can perform them while seeking the fastest time or highest score, in which case we compromise our survival training. Even the IDPA—the best of the shooting sports from a tactical standpoint—falls short of real survival training. This is not a criticism, merely an observation. I commend the IDPA and its founders for bringing a significant amount of tactical realism to what is, and must be, a sport.

Of course, force-on-force drills are another ball of wax. They are as close to tactical realism as we can get. While they offer genuine tactical training and provide objective feedback regarding your survival, they are impossible to judge objectively in a competitive setting. Also—and no one has figured out the solution to this yet—they quickly degenerate into paintball games once the participants realize that they aren't going to die.

Am I condemning sports organizations like IPSC and IDPA? Not at all! I encourage them. In fact, I should take my own advice and participate in them more. What they develop—as few other activities can—are gun-handling skills, which are a vital foundation of real-world shooting. Yes, they can also cause you to develop unsound habits, but they don't have to. If you do ONLY sport shooting, then, of course, in a real situation you'll respond as you've trained—that is, in a tactically unsound manner. But if you do both sport and serious tactical training, there should be no confusion. A case in point: I was in a SWAT course with a highly regarded SWAT officer from a medium-sized city. He is also a nationally ranked master-class IPSC competitor. I asked him if he ever got confused and resorted to IPSC gamesmanship tactics on a raid. "Look," he said, a little perturbed, "When I'm at a match and I have my tricked-out IPSC pistol in my hand, I shoot IPSC-style. When I'm in my tactical uniform, wearing body armor, and carrying my service pistol, I know I'm not at a match, and I act tactically."

So it is possible to practice both sport shooting and tactical shooting. If your emphasis is on survival shooting, don't be afraid to engage in some sport shooting—you can only improve your skill. Just remember not to let the sport techniques become predominant and overwhelm your tactical skills in a real-life confrontation.

1. Edging around the corner in "slices."
2. Fatal funnel refers to an area that you must move through and where you are vulnerable. The most common example is entering a darkened room from a well-lit area—you will be silhouetted by back-light and physically confined by the entrance.

CHAPTER 7

The Problem of Range Standards

One of the bedrock drills of so-called "practical" self-defense training involves waiting for a buzzer cue, drawing, and hitting some sort of A-Zone from 5 to 10 yards. OK, the last time I did this I was somewhere near the normal standard times for this type of exercise. As I recall, I was hitting 9-inch plates at 7 yards in 1.3-something seconds (on the good runs).

Big deal.

I didn't say what caliber I was shooting (it was 9mm), or the gun I was using (a Glock 19), or the sights installed on the pistol (Ashley Big Dot Tritium). I wasn't drawing from concealment, I was standing still, I knew the buzzer was set to go off within a few seconds, and I was prepared and focused on the target. Heck, with a little practice, I probably could have done a cartwheel first and placed the shot in under 4 seconds!

Except for drawing and shooting a gun, I was doing almost nothing realistic. I wasn't moving to cover, or even looking for it. In fact, I wasn't moving at all—something that seems rather unlikely if I was really in the path of an incoming attack. I wasn't reacting to a startle cue, which, if not the street norm, is at least the more prudent "worst case" way to practice. The target wasn't even moving at me.

In short, I was amusing myself, not practicing self-defense. I was measuring myself against a set of arbitrary performance standards that had nothing whatsoever to do with reality, not honing self-preservation skills. I was engaging in sport, not combat.

Now let me be crystal clear. I have nothing whatsoever against this standard exercise. It's useful! But it's a psychomotor exercise, not realistic practice. It's a Stage 2 drill, not Stage 3 training (see Chapter 3, "The Range Effect").

After all, where do standards such as these come from? The truth is that standards like hitting a 9-inch plate at 21 feet in 1.5 seconds exist because they reflect what we CAN do, not what we NEED to do. Consider: if someone is attacking me from 21 feet, they will be on top of me in 1.5 seconds, as we all know from the Tueller drill.[1] Likewise, if I was required to shoot an attacker at 21 feet, he would have to have started the assault at 42 feet to be at 21 feet 1.5 seconds later. Someone assaulting me at 42 feet seems unlikely when we know that most deadly-force encounters happen at 5 feet. The same analysis might be applied to any number of standard routines, such as El Presidente. Further, the "standard" time on these exercises varies by how they are set up. You are given more time to draw from concealment or a fanny pack than from a speed rig, for example. Yet on the street, your assailant doesn't give a damn about these things.

Despite the drawbacks, I'm actually a big fan of many of

these standard exercises. They develop gun handling skills and accurate, fast shooting—things that are undeniably good. We have to keep in mind, however, that they are merely exercises, not reality simulations. They are like practicing scales, not playing music.

Consider this: take your basic A-class or master-class IPSC shooters. I'd personally consider mortgaging the future income of my firstborn to have their skills (if I had a firstborn). But now put them 5 feet from a big, tough, mean street fighter intent on killing them. At this point, I might be able to trade them a couple years of my martial arts training for their entire collection of "wunder guns" and all of their trophy-winning skill.

With standard exercises, we can always improve our times by concentrating on the tools of sight picture, trigger squeeze, a stable stance, etc. Yet on the street, at realistic distances, and under body alarm reaction (see Chapter 8 for more on this subject), it's doubtful if we'll be able to use these fine instruments. There's just too much evidence to the contrary to prudently RELY on them being possible.

A good example of this dichotomy between excellent drills and real situations is the technique of managing trigger reset and riding the recoil between shots on multiple target drills. On the street, facing death at close distance, it's somewhat doubtful you'll be able to finesse your gun in such a way.

If we are to carry and use our guns responsibly, safely, and effectively, we need to be competent, confident, and comfortable with them. Drills such as I've been discussing accomplish these goals well. But after these characteristics have been acquired, we need to move on to realistic street scenarios so that if we do get a chance to employ our gun during them, we will do so with efficacy.

World-class shooting instructor John Farnam is fond of pointing out that tactics, by definition, find the best ways out of the worst situations. Thus, "good tactics" is a contradiction of terms. We do ourselves no favors by mistaking good performance on range-standard exercises for these nonexistent good tactics.

1. In this well-known drill using dummy weapons, a knife-wielding attacker begins charging a gun-carrying defender from 21 feet away. As soon as the defender sees the attacker move, he starts to draw and fire at the attacker. Most people, young or old, can cover the 21 feet in less than 1.5 seconds. It takes about that long to react to the threat and draw and fire. So the Tueller drill has established 21 feet as the generally accepted "safe" distance to be from a person with a knife intent on doing you harm.

CHAPTER 8

Startle Recovery, Point Shooting, and Why They're So Damn Important

There have been several long-running debates in the firearms community over the last 20 years or so. It's tempting to toss sighted vs. point shooting into that same bucket as an irrelevant and artificial debate. Don't do it! The questions at hand have life-and-death consequences. They affect almost everything we do and every way we train for real-life deadly-force encounters with a handgun. We stake our lives on our training, and these two training methods are very far apart indeed. Choosing the training method— or combination of methods—that reflects reality is thus a vitally important task.

The first problem with the debate as it's currently being conducted in the community is that it's gotten political, emotional,

The classic "modern technique" with its sighted fire and stylized posture is losing popularity lately, although it does have its share of real-life proponents.

Point-shooting is making a resurgence these days. It has much to recommend it, having been wrongly snubbed for decades.

and acrimonious, with many big names and big egos (not necessarily the same people) having staked their reputations on their position. The second problem is that so many of these folks do not conduct the debate on the basis of a detailed knowledge of physiology and biochemistry. The third problem is that very few of the people vocal about this subject have actually survived enough gunfights to draw any valid conclusions. The fourth problem is that some very important factors aren't being considered.

I certainly don't know the answer to which method of aiming is better. But I have as great a stake in eventually knowing it as the next shooter. To help the matter along, I list below what we know and what we need to research regarding this vital issue. I mention things that favor point shooting, and things that favor sighted shooting. Some of these items are, or may appear to be, contradictory—that's why we need to invest some real time and real science in discovering the answers.

GENERAL OBSERVATIONS

Undefined Terms

First, let's define terms. We need to understand that there are two variables at play here. Your gun can be in your cone of vision or not, and your focus can be on the sights or on the target. *Sighted shooting* is best defined as using an object in between your eyes and the target to align the gun with the target. Usually one or both sights are so used, but the silhouette of the gun itself may be used, as may some other features of the gun. *Point shooting* is best understood as relying on your "pointing" ability to index the gun to the target. It may be done from the hip, chest height, at eye level, or anywhere at all. *Aimed* shooting is a nebulous term that defies definition, since things as diverse as sight/target alignment and body indexing can be used to "aim" the gun. (Webster's defines "aim" simply as *to direct*.)

Various point shooting advocates hold the gun in different places—some between the eyes and the target, and some not, and therein lies some of the confusion. If by point shooting we mean the Applegate technique,[1] it's uncertain whether this method can be said to also incorporate elements of sighted shooting, since the colonel's method brings the gun up to eye level until it interrupts the line of vision; thus, at least the silhouette of the gun can be visible. So point shooting may not necessarily be "unsighted" shooting. Various popular techniques are plotted in these two dimensions in the graph below (technique placement is based on my own understanding—other people may have different opinions).

As we research and discuss this serious issue, we should therefore take pains to keep our terms as precise as possible.

Alarm Reaction Agreed On

Some facts about high-stress situations are well accepted. Let me quote Stephen P. Wenger, Pharm. D.:

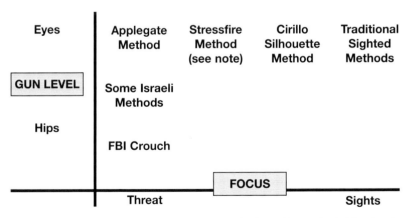

| Eyes | Applegate Method | Stressfire Method (see note) | Cirillo Silhouette Method | Traditional Sighted Methods |

| GUN LEVEL | Some Israeli Methods |

| Hips |

| FBI Crouch |

| | | FOCUS | |
| | Threat | | Sights |

Author's note: I'm unsure as to where to put the Stressfire method. Mas Ayoob describes it clearly as a "target focus" method, yet it relies on seeing the front sight, so I split the difference.

The autonomic nervous system (ANS), which directs our bodily functions without conscious thought, is divided into two basic branches. One, the parasympathetic branch (PANS), is usually associated with things like restoring and maintaining the body. The other, the sympathetic branch (SANS), is usually associated with the fight-or-flight reflex. This is an extremely simple summary; the PANS and SANS have different effects and degrees of influence on different parts of the body. These effects see-saw back and forth as we go through our daily lives. When we are threatened, the effects of the SANS tend to tip the balance to one side. Some people (notably, use-of-force authority Bruce Siddle) have argued that at some point the SANS tips the balance so far that many functions which we would still wish to control with conscious thought become impossible.

So when a spontaneous threat occurs, the SANS tends to dominate the PANS, a condition I call SANS dominance. The term body alarm reaction (or the older term, alarm reaction) refers to this shift toward SANS dominance. Note that SANS dominance is a relative affair. At its mildest levels, SANS dominance occurs when we anticipate something stressful. Its most extreme manifestation occurs if we find ourselves startled by a deadly threat, with no opportunity to prepare for the battle. It is this postulated, extreme SANS dominance which I call SANS override.

At some point along the SANS dominance curve, all the evidence points to the fact that we seem compelled to look at our threat, whether that threat is near or far, and not at our sights. Now, SANS dominance is a complicated phenomenon, comprising several biochemical mechanisms and central nervous system actions. To what extent SANS dominance causes us to immediately lose the ability to focus on near objects such as the front sight (a phenomenon called negative accommodation[2]), presumably through a SANS nerve connection to the ciliary muscle of the eye,[3] and at what point this might occur, is not clear and is a debated topic.

Again, Stephen Wenger:

> In recent years, neuroscientists have become increasingly aware of the role of a very small structure at the base of the forebrain, called the amygdala. The top of the forebrain is the cerebral cortex or "thinking brain," while the amygdala is the "emotional brain." When the amygdala is activated by something we have learned to fear, it tends to overwhelm the cerebral cortex. It is this part of the brain which activates the SANS in response to threats. Thus, any interference with bodily functions which appears to be related to the dominance of the SANS is, in fact, initiated by the activation of the amygdala, which is also reaching out to other portions of the brain simultaneously. If we realize that the SANS is only an extension of the central nervous system (CNS) and in some circumstances, of the amygdala, we may better understand why we focus on a threat which triggers our emotional response, WHETHER THAT PERCEIVED THREAT IS 2 FEET AWAY OR 20 FEET AWAY. If we have reacted with the emotional brain, the rest of the brain may no longer appreciate the need to focus on the front sight. Because the emotional brain has

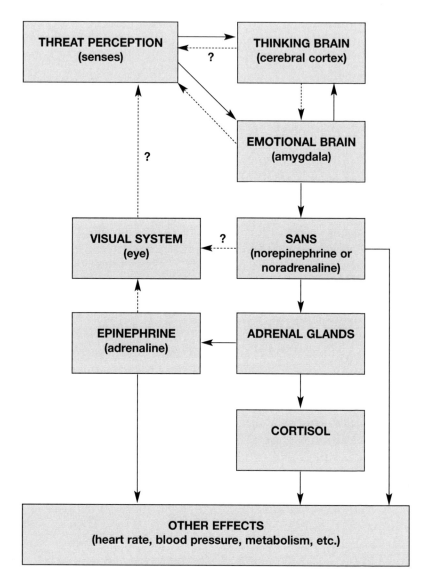

LEGEND: ——————— Major Pathways

 ------------------- Minor Pathways

 ? Speculative Pathways

A gun stuck in your face. If your eyes couldn't focus at near distances under stress, you wouldn't be able to see the gun clearly. Under stress, you focus on the threat—wherever it is.

the power to overwhelm the thinking brain, it most likely is involved in filtering our perceptions and producing things like tachypsychia (slowing of time), tunnel vision, and auditory exclusion (seeming deafness).

On the previous page is a simplified diagram of what happens (diagram courtesy of Stephen Wenger):

The epinephrine release of the adrenal glands does not seem to cause negative accommodation. Recent experiments by Mas Ayoob suggest that epinephrine by itself does not, in fact, cause loss of near focus—the subjects in that experiment were perfectly capable of focusing on their front sights under the effects of injected epinephrine (at least at the dosages involved.) Note, however, that epinephrine release is but one of the effects of SANS dominance, and injecting ourselves with epinephrine does not mimic the full effects of SANS dominance, let alone full-blown SANS override. Further, epinephrine release is a bloodstream phenomenon—taking circulation time to affect the eye—and not immediately acting.

Threat Focus, Not Far Focus?

Where, then, does the tendency to look at the threat come from if not from epinephrine or a SANS nerve connection to the ciliary muscle? We must suspect that it is the mind itself (not the eyes) that insists on focusing entirely on the threat, rather than the sights. Aside from the fact that this is often the right tactical thing to do, it's innate: every instinct and survival mechanism tells us to focus on the threat—to look at the person trying to kill us so we can respond to his actions. When our lives are threatened, we look at the thing or person causing the threat. We have millions of years of hard-wiring telling us to do just that in a fight. Indeed, the right thing to do if unarmed, or armed with any weapon but a firearm, is to concentrate on the threat. Trying to look at your sights in such situations is likely to be counter to millions of years of evolutionary natural selection.

This tunnel-vision/target-focusing phenomenon is apparent to anyone who has ever used the old Motorola Shoot/Don't Shoot training videos. While watching the small TV screen on which these videos play, it is extremely common for trainees to focus entirely on the person in the picture "threatening them" and miss a second lethal threat—which is only inches away on the screen. So clearly, threat focus is not a matter of visual focus but something the mind is doing.

The compulsion to look at the threat is not the same thing as negative accommodation; we seem to be able to focus on and see near threats, too. Consider victim reports of seeing in extreme detail a gun pointed at them, while not seeing clearly the face of the perpetrator a good 2-3 feet further away. The attacker's face would be easier to focus on if we did in fact lose the ability to see near objects under SANS dominance.

The foregoing doesn't imply that we can use our sights under SANS dominance. It simply suggests that what SANS dominance may induce is threat focus, not far focus.

Lack of Data

We really don't have any scientific data about what happens to people under the effects of SANS dominance trying to shoot at someone, nor do we have a reliable way to measure the degree of SANS dominance in people under fire, which is a critical factor. All we really have are stories. Given the dozens (at least) of variables involved in such a situation, we'd need many thousands of identically conducted post-event interviews to arrive at some halfway reasonable conclusions. This is not at all impossible to do—a simple federal grant of modest proportions might be enough. It would require, however, that experts in the field of SANS dominance biochemistry and experts in statistical data collection be involved. It would require real science. As far as I know, none of the people who've published in this area in the law enforcement or firearms press have a true scientific background in these areas.

Startle Recovery

It seems common sense to suspect that people who are highly trained can recover from being startled and recover from SANS dominance (or perhaps abort it) very quickly. Bruce Siddle is of the opinion that the lower the degree of SANS dominance, the easier this can be. He is also of the opinion that it is all but impossible to recover quickly from full-blown SANS override (and also perhaps undesirable, due to the PANS backlash that follows SANS—which can be likened to a "sugar crash from hell" that can leave you in an even less fit state to fight than SANS override). I suspect that we've been teaching a form of SANS recovery in the street-realistic martial arts.[4] I call this phenomenon *startle recovery*.

Lack of Respectable Science

Much of the "research" and metaresearch in this area is self-published and written by authors without a hard science background. It is not peer-reviewed, and is sponsored by individuals or organizations with a political and/or economic stake in promoting their point of view. While much of the training that comes from these endeavors is valuable and practical, this is not the way real science is done, and we risk error by depending on them.

Reasonable Targets

The issue at hand here is whether sighted or point fire is a better survival strategy in a real firefight. Firing at static, flat paper targets on a nice, flat, comfortable range is not an appropriate way to determine this. If we are going to compare the effectiveness of sighted vs. point fire, and we're constrained to doing so on a traditional range, we should be using something like the Rogers Range. This range more closely mimics the real-life fast, moving, target acquisition skills that we'll have to use for real in any nontrivial scenario. It consists of multiple moving steel plates that pop into view at random times at various distances for short intervals. This is a very, very humbling machine to shoot, and it gives us a better indication of how our skills relate to a difficult street-survival situation.

No Point-Shooting Data

The most relevant fact in this entire discussion is that we simply have no *completely* valid statistical data on the performance of point-trained shooters in actual combat (although the experience of the California Highway Patrol is very close—see the section later in this chapter on the CHP). Too few people have been trained in point shooting recently to have gotten into many recorded and appropriately debriefed gunfights, and there is always the problem of keeping track of whether point-trained shooters have also had exposure to sighted-fire instruction or practice, etc. It's been suggested that since point shooting was practiced for so many years prior to the '60s, data from this earlier period—if it's available—would be relevant here.

Hard to Miss

Point shooting, at least Applegate-style point shooting, was designed for close-in work. Since 54 percent of gunfights happen within 5 feet[5] and 74 percent happen within 10 feet, no one on either side of this debate argues that Applegate-style point shooting shouldn't be reasonably accurate at these close ranges. Indeed, many sighted curricula teach a form of point shooing at these close distances. The mystery is why so many shooters miss at these ranges (the hit ratio reported in most law enforcement studies is less than 20 percent).

To the extent that point shooting instruction has shown better results (see the section on the CHP), it must be partially due to better quality instructional methods coupled with the point-shooting instruction, including the use of one hand at close distances.[6]

The Need for Accuracy

Some folks on the point-shooting side of the debate take issue with the need for traditional accuracy standards. It's always been my opinion (not my skill level) that combat accuracy is the ability to hit an 8-inch circle or an 8 1/2 x 11-inch piece of paper from wherever you are. In support of this position, let me quote Bert DuVernay, the director of the Smith & Wesson Academy:

> I don't know of any hard data here, as such, since there is a shortage of volunteers willing to be shot in a controlled manner. What we do know is that everyone (to my knowledge) that has made a serious study of "stopping power" has concluded that the only two ways to stop determined attackers with handgun rounds are 1) Central Nervous System (CNS) hits, and 2) dropping the blood pressure with large and numerous Cardiovascular System (CVS) hits. Common agreement goes further to the fact that since the skull is difficult to penetrate reliably with handgun rounds, the preferential approach is with the CVS.
>
> This information is agreed upon by the even the most diametrically opposed students of the issue. Marshall refers to it in his first book on stopping power,[7] and language to the same effect is included in the introduction of the first FBI ammo tests book.[8] Dr. (Martin) Fackler[9] has made similar references in articles (but I don't know of any text in which he says it directly). Dave Spaulding (a lieutenant with the Montgomery County, Ohio, Sheriff's Office), whose master's thesis was on the subject, has made similar statements. Vince DiMaio (former medical examiner of Bexar County, Texas) has personally made similar statements to me in conversation. He characterized stopping power as "where they're hit and the number of times they're hit," clearly

indicated at the time as a reference to CVS hits and hypovolemic shock.

I don't know of any serious student of the issue that makes any other argument. I have heard people who should know better make statements to the contrary, but when challenged on the matter will invariably beg off either by saying that they really haven't researched "stopping power" that much or by saying that it is an unrealistic training standard from a normative sense, sidestepping the physiological issue completely. I am not a believer in normative standards for LE training. Either you can meet job related requirements or you can't. If the standards can be normed, they aren't job related.

Therefore, since A) every serious student of the issue that I know of has come to the same conclusion, B) they can explain the mechanism of collapse logically and in detail, and C) detractors of the theory cannot offer any meaningful alternative, I conclude that, notwithstanding circumstances that permit skull penetration, multiple hits to the CVS, nominally 8 inches in size, are required to reliably and (fairly) rapidly incapacitate a determined attacker.

To give fair play to the other point of view, this is not to say that noncenter mass or non-CNS hits aren't useful. Certainly many fights have been won because the winner's first such shot put the loser behind the power curve. In fact, the point-shooter's reply to the above is that hits anywhere on the torso, delivered as fast as possible, are what win fights. And without regard to where they eventually land, rounds that entirely miss our adversary may be of value in a gunfight, too—after all, no one likes to be shot at.

Since you must incapacitate an assailant quicker at close range than at longer ranges, we can argue that greater accuracy is required (all else being equal) the closer the distance. However, since we are presumed to be shooting defensively, we are probably reacting to our assailant's assault and are already well behind the power curve in the reaction-time dominated dynamics of a close-in gunfight. Thus, our speed is of the utmost importance, and many rapidly delivered shots to the torso can be argued to be more efficacious than a slower, more precise series of shots. But it can also be argued that it will take several seconds for a determined attacker to be stopped by even the most precisely delivered handgun rounds, and that the fractions of a second saved by not sighting all pale in importance to the critical issue of delivering for-sure stopping shots.

The point of all this is determining the standards we're willing to accept in our training and our reasoning for doing so.

ADVANTAGES OF POINT SHOOTING

Interesting historical note: Question: "How did you kill those men? What was your method or technique?" Wild Bill Hickok's answer: "I raised my hand to eye level, like pointing a finger, and fired."

Physiological Reactions

Body alarm reaction induces crouching, muscle tensing, and target square-off. So the target focus, crouch, target facing, and convulsive grip of Applegate-style point shooting is in line with the physiological aspects of body alarm reaction. (A slightly crouched, two-handed isosceles stance seems also to conform to body alarm reaction.)

About to initiate the action by entering the room, this officer may not suffer the effects of SANS override.

Common Sense

To suggest that we will be able to force ourselves to look at our front sight—let alone align the front and rear sights—when someone is trying to kill us flies in the face of common sense, our own emergency situation experiences, and the experience of many people who've been there. We see this repeatedly when students first use simulators (like FATS and CAPS machines), as well as when they go through Simunitions exercises. (Eventually students can learn to focus on the front sight during a simulated exercise, but this only happens once they realize that they aren't in any danger whatsoever.) Even highly respected sighted shooting advocate, combat veteran, and world-class instructor John Farnam has been known to resort to one-handed point fire during Simunitions scenarios at the National Tactical Invitational.

Foreknowledge Matters

Reports from the field by trained people who've faced hostile fire include both those that saw their front sight clearly and those who don't remember it at all. Digging a little deeper into this admittedly anecdotal evidence, it seems that those who had the advantage of foreknowledge of a shooting (perhaps by only a second, as when challenging a suspect), distance, or preparation and surprise (like a SWAT entry) were the most likely to see their sights.[10] Those who were taken by surprise tended to not see their sights and looked at the threat. A working hypothesis might be that trained people who have foreknowledge of a possible shooting (even a fraction of a second) are able to control their body alarm reaction onset and thus not suffer from SANS dominance to the degree that they might otherwise. We should also note here the anecdotal evidence of threat focus occurring during law enforcement raids when things didn't go according to plan (as in "Oh S#@&!).

Pointing Can Be Accurate

I've had experience with point shooting—defined as gun at shoulder level—giving me accuracy (easily 8-inch groups) out to 12 yards when I maintained total, Zen-like focus on the target. The moment I even thought of my gun, the groups opened way up. But this was on a nice, controlled range.

Gross Motor Skills

In the unarmed self-defense/defensive-tactics area it is virtually gospel that we need to rely on simple gross motor skills, and not fine and/or complex motor skills, because the latter fail under real-life conditions for all but the extremely highly trained. Sighted shooting is a complex and fine motor skill. How can we profess the validity of relying only on simple gross motor skills under stress when we're unarmed and still advocate relying on fine complex motor skills when we're armed?

Unrealistic Sighted Practice

Traditional sighted shooting instruction is on static paper targets on a safe, controlled range. This traditional training has almost no relevance to a real life-or-death encounter. If sighted shooting instructors are really teaching survival skills, they must introduce the elements of surprise, movement, uneven terrain, startle, and human opponents into their students' training—all of which is possible with Simunitions. What is also necessary, but isn't possible, is introducing actual danger into this training. Without actual danger, inducing SANS dominance is problematic.

Dim Light

Most defensive gunshots are fired in dim-light conditions. In all but virtually no-light conditions, it is possible to identify a (hostile) target, but in many dim-light conditions, it is impossible to see your sights at the same time. Therefore, unless sighted-fire advocates both 1) have tritium night sights on their guns, and 2) practice extensively in dim light with them, they are fooling themselves, because they are going to have to use point fire in an actual situation. Point shooting will also be necessary if one is blinded in any circumstance, such as coming from a dark room into bright sunlight.

Flash Sight Picture

Even the dean of sighted shooters, Jeff Cooper, teaches that at high skill levels the shooter relies on "muscle memory" (i.e., a highly refined pointing ability) to put the gun on target and uses a "flash sight picture," not to align the gun with the target, but to confirm that the gun is already on target. This sounds damn-near Applegate-style point shooting to me.

Invisible Sights

We must suspect the reports of people seeing their sights under stress. Recall the experiment done at the Sigarms Academy a few years ago in which students were issued a holstered gun and put in role-playing scenarios. Many students recalled seeing their sights even though the issued gun had no sights! On the other hand, it's not unusual for a gunfight survivor to not remember reloading, either. John Farman reports that he regularly makes distance shots at the the National Tactical Invitational (a high-stress environment) without recalling using his sights, even though he couldn't have hit the target without doing do.

Training Effect

Point shooters tend to do more realistic, close-in training than sighted shooters. Perhaps that has accustomed them to this kind of scenario, and they are better able to control their SANS dominance during a for-real event. After all, hitting a man-sized target at 5 feet is hardly the stuff of superhuman skill under normal conditions—we'd expect almost any shooter, of almost any skill level, trained in any way, to be able to do it. Perhaps the abysmal street hit rates we've seen with sighted-trained shooters are simply due to lack of sufficient realistic practice at close ranges.

Didn't See or Didn't Remember?

We don't know if sighted-trained shooters who reported not seeing their sights in a firefight actually didn't see them or simply didn't remember seeing them. Is it possible that they saw them fuzzily and aligned them with their assailant? We don't know.

The closer the threat, the more likely you are to experience SANS override. (Photo by Penny Harris.)

Distance

There are two arguments commonly used against point shooting by sighted-shooting advocates: 1) Everyone in the debate seems to agree that at "longer" distances—usually past 10 or 15 yards, sighted shooting must be employed in order to ensure hits. But how can point-shooting advocates advise using the sights past 10 yards if we cannot see the sights in a life-and-death encounter? 2) If we are incapable of using our sights during a life-or-death encounter, as the point-shooting advocates would have us believe, then of course we are unable to use them no matter what weapon we're holding. Therefore, to be logically consistent, these advocates should be arguing for point-shooting a rifle. This is clearly a silly notion at rifle distances.

The answer that point-shooting advocates give to these arguments is that the farther you are from an assailant the less you suffer from SANS dominance. Bruce Siddle suggests that the components necessary for a SANS override are surprise, close distance, and a deadly-force threat. This certainly appeals to common sense, since throughout most of man's history, only something close to you was capable of killing you.

ADVANTAGES OF SIGHTED SHOOTING

Interesting historical note: Bat Masterson, explaining why a man won a gunfight: "He looked through the sights of his pistol, which is a very essential thing do when shooting at an adversary who is returning your fire."

Pointing Inaccurate

In many instructors' experience, Applegate-style point shooting allows you to score only 12-inch+ groups out to 7 yards at moderate speeds. This is not the 15 yards Colonel Applegate claimed point shooting is accurate to (I understand that his definition of "accurate" was making head shots), nor is it the 8-inch groups experts generally agree is necessary for stopping effectiveness. (Experiments at Hocking College do show, however, that from a low ready it's possible to get point-shooting hits on an 8 1/2 x 11-inch target from 10 feet. Reasonably accurate hits at this distance from a static position are hardly surprising.) Further, in my experience, the demonstrations of point shooting by its advocates are generally neither from the holster nor against a moving suspect, both of which are the rule when drawing from a startle response against a real attacker.

No Set Heart Rate

Claims that the SANS is inevitably activated to a particular degree at a given heart rate (usually cited as 145 beats per minute) are highly suspect. It is true that SANS does raise the heart rate (sometimes dramatically), but it's the SANS dominance that's the cause, not the effect. Further, common sense tells us that the relationship must vary with age, physical condition, mental conditioning, and so on. There are certainly instances of operators performing fine and/or complex motor skills at much higher heart rates.

But controlling heart rate as a means of controlling SANS dominance does seem like a fruitful approach to the problem, since the two are linked. We know that heart rate can be controlled through concentration and other mechanisms—indeed, this is a well known stress-management technique.

Unrealistic Point Training

Like other kinds of firearms instruction, "point shooting" training is conducted using static paper targets on a safe, controlled range. So this training also has almost no relevance to a real life-or-death encounter. Again, if instructors really want to teach survival skills, they must introduce the elements of surprise, movement, uneven terrain, startle, and human opponents into their students' training. Also, few people would argue that point shooting is as accurate as sighted shooting at small targets, and the fact that the bad guys can be behind cover needs to be taken into account.

Interrupted Vision

Some of the anecdotal evidence from gunfight survivors suggests that having a large front sight that contrasted significantly with the environment—like the old red-insert revolver front sights or the newer Ashley sights—was a determining factor in being able to see the sights. It seems that these "hard to ignore" sights interrupted their field of vision. But did they use them or just notice them? We don't know.

Missed Shots

Going into court to defend yourself when your missed shot hits an innocent person is going to be a difficult task if you fired without sighting. One counter I've heard goes, "You aren't justified in shooting if you aren't in fear of your life. If you're in fear of your life then, because of SANS override, you won't see the sights."

In any case, it certainly does appear to be completely irresponsible to shoot a gun in public without using the sights. A gun is a deadly weapon, with an accompanying level of responsibility attached to it. It's irresponsible to argue that point shooting should be taught simply because learning to use sighted fire under stress in the allocated class time is beyond the average person. No matter how much time it takes, every type of firearms training must teach the shooter to be safe and responsible with that lethal tool.

Military Training

Colonel Applegate's technique was devised for training large numbers of previously untrained men, using guns that had feeble sights, and often with only part of a day to devote to firearms skills. His was a brilliant method to accomplish that objective. A vital distinction to keep in mind, however, is that he was training soldiers for war, where misses and "collateral damage" (i.e., injuring innocent people) were perfectly acceptable; in peace-time civilian life, misses (and the innocent people they hit) aren't.[11]

Squared to Target

Applegate-style point shooting is based on being squared to the target. In real life, multiple assailants are increasingly the rule—everybody's moving and all hell is breaking loose. If point-shooting accuracy is dependent on staying squared to the target, then it suffers from a real-life deficiency.[12]

Higher Level Skills

The consensus among instructors I've talked with is that point-trained shooters do very poorly in any skill other than shooting at close-in full-torso targets. In order to progress to intermediate and higher level firearms skills, they have to be retooled in sighted fire.

Fighter Pilots, Etc.

There are copious examples of people performing highly complex skills under life-and-death stress—fighter pilots, for example. Obviously these people are not under the effects of SANS override, or are not debilitated by it if they are. However, these pilots know they're going into action when they take off—they aren't surprised when they have to fight. They are also highly trained and highly physically fit. So clearly it's possible to train ourselves to engage in a life-or-death situation and remain reasonably calm (martial artists do this all the time).

Consider the case of FBI Agent Ed Mireles, the hero of the infamous Miami gunfight in 1986. If ever there was a candidate for being in SANS override, it's him! Yet he reports that his strongest memory was seeing the front sight on his revolver as he delivered the telling five fatal shots of that encounter.[13]

Motivation

It seems logical that the motivation of the people involved will make a big difference in the outcome. An elite forces volunteer with the mind-set to go with the job will probably fare much better under combat stress than your basic donut cop who took the job for the civil service pension. Certainly your basic navy SEAL will be better able to control SANS dominance, and will have better startle recovery, than Joe Bagadonuts.

Sighted Training May Provide Point Skill

Logic and experience indicate that if we train in sighted shooting to an acceptable level we'll also develop the kinesthetic alignment (the so-called "muscle memory") to point shoot with reasonable accuracy. Much of the failure of sighted-trained shooters in real-life encounters may be due to their marginal training at realistic close distances, at which they developed sufficient skill in neither sighted accuracy nor its potentially logical spin-off, point accuracy. I've never seen a breakdown of the hit rates of real-life encounters that factored the results by training level. Another interesting possibility is that under the extreme speed and stress of a deadly attack from 10 feet (at which distance they've never realistically trained), traditionally trained shooters may obtain a poor grip on their gun, which will contribute to missed shots.

FIELD EXPERIENCE

Training Makes a Difference

New York Police Department (NYPD) data indicates that department hit rates have climbed from roughly the national average of 17 percent to 30-40 percent (in 1994) due to increased sighted shooting training. Data from the well-schooled-in-sighted-fire Los Angeles Police Department (LAPD) indicates a 40+ percent hit ratio (and both cities report much higher hit rates—in the vicinity of 80 percent—for the better-trained special units).

Hocking College

Hocking College's experience in teaching police recruits the point-shooting method is highly touted. The description of moving from sighted shooting to point shooting in *Bullseyes Don't Shoot Back* (Col. Rex Applegate and Michael D. Janich, Paladin Press, 1998, pp. 73-90) is often cited, but it is not a good comparative example of the two methods.[14]

More instructive is the later data, reported to me in February 1999. The college had previously taught the Cooper-style "modern technique" for recruits—Weaver stance and all. The average qualifying score for 320 students taught this way from 1980 to 1986 was 88.5 percent. After transitioning to a curriculum that includes Applegate-style point shooting, the average score for 160 students from 1996 to 1997 was 93.6 percent. The same course of fire was used throughout.

The earlier students qualified on the target mandated by the Ohio Peace Officer Training Council (OPOTC). It scores two points for hitting an approximately 2-feet by 1-foot area and one point for hitting anywhere (even the arms) on a groin-and-up face-on silhouette of an average male. This is a very generous qualifying target. Also used in the earlier group was the NRA B-27 target, with two points scored for any hit within the 7-ring (an area measuring 23 x 15.5 inches) and one point scored for hitting the target outside the 7-ring.

The point-trained shooters used the OPOTC target and the NYC Transit PD target, with a slightly smaller scoring area. Time standards were typical (generous) police qualification times for both groups.

The highly motivated and qualified Hocking staff is convinced that its present course of instruction is far superior to the old method for many reasons, including student retention and learning time. However, we can't really draw any firm conclusions from the Hocking experience to date for the following reasons:

- The obvious change of targets makes strict comparisons impossible.
- The sequence of instruction also changed. The Modern Technique shooters started their shooting education at 50 yards and progressed forward, while the point-trained shooters start at the target and progress back—which is generally conceded to be a superior method of introducing a new student to a handgun.
- Consider that the Modern Technique, with its Weaver stance and all of its other difficult-to-master elements, is a very poor baseline to begin with. Simply put, almost no one teaches this approach to police recruits anymore, since A) it's so difficult to master, and B) without a pretty high level of training and practice it often falls apart during real-life events. Virtually all police trainers now teach the isosceles stance to beginners. (Even most competitive shooters use the isosceles now, although there are some extremely highly regarded instructors—John Farnam and Clint Smith among them—who teach the Weaver.)
- Eighty-eight percent of the course of fire is 20 feet or less. This is a pretty short distance, and most people on both sides of this debate concede that unsighted fire has a pretty good chance of hitting a reasonably-sized static target at this distance.
- The longest shot here is from 50 feet, but this is done with sighted fire.
- One-handed, Applegate-style point shooting was only

used from 10 feet, while hip shooting was used at 3 feet. This is not different from many traditional sighted-fire curricula which also teach "point-shoulder" unsighted fire at 3 yards and hip shooting at 3 feet.

- Eye-level shooting using the isosceles stance is used at intermediate distances. Unsighted fire is encouraged at these distances, but how can that be enforced?
- The difference between the sighted shooters' average score of 88.5 percent and the point-shooters' average score of 93.6 percent is really quite small, especially in light of all of the variables involved.

What the Hocking experience does show is that within 3.3 yards, the average police recruit can hit a 1-by-2-foot area most of the time using Applegate and hip point-shooting techniques. Against a nonmoving, face-on target, on a flat controlled range, this result is not really surprising.

The same problems that make an apples-to-apples comparison impossible at Hocking College—changing targets, lack of accurate comparative data, instructional changes, etc.—also afflict many other departments that have incorporated point shooting into their training. I simply have not been able to find a properly controlled experiment, with a suitable control group and all other factors normalized, with which to compare even the range results of virgin shooters. And, of course, these range results are only a proxy for actual street results against live, thinking, moving targets.

CHP

The California Highway Patrol recently changed its entire training curriculum to incorporate point shooting. Troops trained with the traditional, bull's-eye focused methods had been seeing street hit rates at about 15 percent. But the firefights involving officers trained with the new method show an astounding jump to more than 90 percent at typical gunfight distances. These fights were generally at close ranges, and the officers involved are reporting that they reacted as trained (i.e., they point-shot).

That's great news. It certainly shows that Applegate-style point shooting works at close ranges. But other things changed besides the introduction of point shooting. To begin with, the course of fire (including the targets), as well as the entire method of instruction were changed. The new curriculum[15] put together by Lou Chiodo is a model of modern street-relevant training, and it is superior in every way to the old curriculum. This obviously means that we can't compare qualification scores between the old and new methods (in addition, the new system demands 100-percent performance at each stage, and an officer is remedied on the spot until he

Lou Chiodo is the man responsible for revamping the CHP's firearms program. The new program has resulted in an outstanding record of hits in the agency's many gunfights.

or she can meet this standard—so there is no other qualification score other than "100"). It also means that we have a hard time sorting out the causes of the vast improvement in street hit rates.

Lou also reports that his shooters engage the target much faster at realistic combat distances using point shooting, they are learning to shoot faster, and they report increased confidence in their abilities over the old system.

Certainly if the 90-percent hit rate continues, then Lou and CHP are definitely onto the right stuff!

Anchorage PD

In conversations with the staff at the Anchorage, Alaska, Police Department, a 90-percent street hit rate is cited. I've been unable to verify this (or the average gunfight distance) as of the deadline for this book, but I have no reason to disbelieve it, either. The interesting thing about this department is that it trains exclusively with the modern technique! But it does a lot of other things differently than most departments, too. To begin with, their academy recruit population includes a high number of military veterans, retired military personnel, or officers transferring from other agencies. The pay is excellent, so the agency can afford to be *very* selective. In the academy, 84 hours are spent on the range—about double the average in my neck of the woods. Further, realistic force-on-force drills (with Simunitions) are incorporated into this training. A great deal of emphasis is also placed on mind-set, and each officer's Glock is equipped with tritium sights. Once out of the academy, each officer receives 1 1/2 hours per month of regular in-service firearms training—1 1/2 hours per month more than at most agencies.

So Anchorage has a selective, motivated pool of officers who receive realistic training. Certainly these factors have as great an impact on their street results as the particular shooting method taught.

Classified Knowledge?

Some folks have pointed out that since the military has classified data on many aspects of combat, there may be a lot more known about this subject than we're aware of.

CONCLUSION/STARTLE RECOVERY

Many skilled shooters on both sides of this debate have told me that they think the Cirillo silhouette method has great merit; if there's any common ground, this may be it. My own experience is that I naturally use this method *when the target is large*—such as most police qualification targets and those used in many simulator scenarios (CAPS, FATS). The smaller the target, the more I look at my sights, even to the point of naturally closing one eye at longer distances. Of course, these are merely range exercises, and I don't get 8-inch groups with a target focus (but then, I'm not that good a shooter). I should also point out that many top competitive shooters are on record as employing target focus rather than sight focus.

Several other things jump out at me from all this—besides the fact that we really need some serious scientific investigation into the whole matter.

A) We should plan on being startled in a life-or-death encounter, and ideally develop the ability to react appropriately, however far the inevitable SANS dominance has progressed—including to SANS override. Given the fact that most encounters are within arm's reach and in dim light, we all need to have point-shooting skills. If we have trained with them, we are more likely to have them work for us in a real situation.

B) We know that sighted fire can be effective and accurate; if you align the sights and press the trigger, you'll hit your target. Sometimes sighted fire is the only way to make a life-saving stop. Therefore we all need to be skilled in sighted fire for those critical times when it is necessary.

C) We tend to focus more and more on the threat as we progress along the SANS dominance curve, so if we can control SANS dominance, we can allow people to use sighted fire more often (when appropriate).

D) The rational people on both sides of this debate really seem to be in agreement on some of the central issues. All agree that past a certain distance sighted fire is necessary, and many seem to agree that at typical gunfight distances (5 feet and less), point fire is appropriate. The debate seems to be 1) about how much we train in point fire vs. sighted fire and out to what distance and 2) what constitutes acceptable accuracy. In any gunfight, there is an inherent trade-off between speed and accuracy. The sighted-shooting advocates prefer to trade off speed for accuracy, while the point-shooters prefer the converse bargain.

Someone needs to compile some realistic statistics on the maximum percentage of good hits that we can expect from well-trained people while they are under life-threatening stress and while they and their opponents are probably in motion. We need to understand what this percentage is and realize that training beyond it will have diminishing returns (not zero return, but diminishing returns). Training time might therefore be better spent on instilling awareness discipline and startle recovery[16]—the ability to control SANS dominance—rather than marksmanship after that point.

There are enough people who seem to have mastered startle recovery or control of SANS dominance—martial artists, elite soldiers, etc.—to think that it's a reasonable goal. Many people on both sides of this issue believe that scenario-based training (using Simunitions) accomplishes this goal to a large degree.

While the true scientific questions about this debate are being sorted out and the field data is coming in, maybe startle recovery—and the scenario-based training that it implies—is the area we ought to be concentrating on.

1. In the rest of this book, we'll be referring to the Applegate method when we use the term point shooting. This method is the most popular of all nonsighted methods, and has the validity of actual field use by many people. We won't consider any of the long-discredited hip-shooting methods. (Please, no one bring up Bill Jordan. If you have his God-given talents and are willing to practice as much as he did, then feel free to hip-shoot.)

2. Accommodation is the process of focusing for close vision. Loss of accommodation would be the inability to focus for close vision. Negative accommodation is focus for far vision (infinity focus).

3. The ciliary muscle controls the amount of flex in the curvature of the eye lens, and thus controls the distance at which your eye is focused.

4. Some martial arts teachers specialize in this. The best known in the law enforcement community are probably Tony Blauer and Shane Steinkemp.

5. We must remember, however, that some of the shooting data we have are based on self-reports. This data may be skewed by two factors: 1) under stress, distances are foreshortened; 2) there is self-interest in reporting an assailant as being as close as reasonably possible, so as to maximize the imminent danger.

6. Note the objection that some instructors have to extending the weapon to your opponent at close distances. It makes a disarm fairly easy (if you're not shooting).

7. *Handgun Stopping Power: The Definitive Study* by Evan P. Marshall and Edwin J. Sanow, available from Paladin Press.

8. *Ammunition Tests 1989*, Firearms Training Unit, FBI Academy, Quantico, Virginia, January 1990.

9. Fackler, an M.D., is the editor of the *Journal of the International Wound Ballistics Association*.

10. The experience of the famed NYC Stakeout Squad of the '60s, including that of its most famous member, Jim Cirillo, seems to be of this variety (most fights happened with the foreknowledge of the good guys). Indeed, they determined that accurate sighted shooting was a determining factor in their success (see *Guns, Bullets and Gunfights*, Jim Cirillo, Paladin Press.) In many cases, they had only small exposed targets to shoot (back) at.

11. Note that Allied operatives were also taught to move about with their fingers inside the trigger guards of cocked 1911A1 .45 pistols! This is an unacceptable practice by today's standards.

12. The CHP saw this as a deficiency, and incorporate non-squared point shooting at close distances.

13. There a certain class of people—on both sides of the badge—who simply don't care whether they live or die. They have true *mushin,* or "no-mind" in these circumstances, and thus remain utterly calm in the face of death. They are, however, the rare exception.

14. For example, the sample size is too small to be significant. Also, this class of recruits had been trained in sighted shooting for the previous several weeks and shot the point-shooting course with their sights on the gun, but taped over. How much the sighted training affected their point-shooting scores we'll never know; likewise with how much the taped-over front sight was used.

15. It's interesting to note that to date, the CHP curriculum has not included Simunitions scenario-based training. This is being introduced, however, as this is written.

16. It has been suggested that Col. Jeff Cooper's color codes are a form of startle recovery. This has some truth to it. The color codes certainly act as a form of startle prevention or startle attenuation, but adhering to them is not the same thing as engaging in explicit exercises to learn to control SANS dominance.

CHAPTER 9

Thou Shalt Not Laser
Thoughts and Techniques Regarding the Ubiquitous "Laser" Safety Violation

At a national conference a couple years ago, I was starting to tell a famous instructor—one I not only like but have tremendous respect for—about Jim Murnak's original and innovative cross-draw holster for women. I was cut off short: "We don't believe in cross-draws," she said, "You wind up lasering your off-side arm every time you draw from it." Well, that ended that part of the conversation, but it sure got me thinking.

[Review for newbies: "Lasering" is the act of letting the muzzle of your unholstered gun point toward anything you wouldn't want to destroy—like one of your own body parts, or those of an innocent person. You visualize this by pretending there's a laser in the muzzle of your gun that will burn anything it touches. Avoiding laser-ing is one of the four cardinal rules of firearms safety.[1]]

THERE'S NO FIRING LINE ON THE STREET

First, there is no reason you have to laser your arm when you draw from a cross-draw holster. Many instructors teach that the nondrawing hand goes in front of the sternum area during any kind of draw, and there it meets the drawing hand once the gun is clear of the holster. Either that, or they teach the more realistic technique of your off-side arm being raised in a defensive position to deal with the likely situation of a close attacker. In either case, drawing from a concealed cross-draw holster often involves clearing the concealing gar-ment with the off-side hand, which often removes it from the lasering danger area. Besides, we've taught nonlasering shoulder holster draws for years, and a shoulder holster is essentially just an uncomfortable cross-draw holster. Finally, the cross-draw holster is often the only practical and com-fortable concealed-carry alternative for many women. If at all possible, it behooves us to teach techniques that will work for the way our students actually carry their weapons.

Second, in a real encounter, we probably will laser some innocent party or ourselves. Remember: there's no firing line on the street, and there will undoubtedly be innocents down-range when you need to shoot. Lasering them as you bring your gun on target will often be simply unavoidable in a real encounter. That's why there are three other cardinal rules of firearms safety! So even if a cross-draw did imply our laser-ing ourselves, I'm not sure we need to automatically discard the technique if there are good reasons to use it. I'm not advocating that we ignore the four safety rules, but rather pointing out that at times we must make trade-offs. Consider: in hunting, a missed or through-and-through shot is a very real possibility. That shot can easily travel over a

This may be a little exaggerated, but most shooters consistently "laser" themselves while reholstering. Watch next time you're on the range!

mile, and to suggest that every hunter "be sure of his back-stop" for that distance is ludicrous.

WHOOPS!

Third, and the real point here: all of us constantly laser ourselves during practice. Every shooter and every instructor I've ever seen angles the gun in toward his or her body while replacing the gun in the strong-side holster. I'm sure you do, too. Watch yourself in a mirror. Folks, we are being hypocritical!

"Ah, ah, ah, duh, duh . . . that's not much of an angle. I mean I'm not really pointing the gun at myself—at least not much," you say? Well, it may not be much of an angle but you're probably lasering your lower pelvis, your thigh, or at least your femoral artery. If not, you're the first person I've ever seen who isn't, and I've watched the biggest names in the business as well as raw beginners do this consistently. There are many accidents each year because of people shooting themselves while reholstering. Just ask Rich Davis of Second Chance Body Armor. He designed and sells a Kevlar Level IIA holster as a direct result of the number of police officers alone who shoot themselves while reholstering. While these people's guns wouldn't have gone off if their fingers had been off the triggers (another cardinal safety rule), they also wouldn't have wound up shooting themselves if their guns hadn't been pointed at them.

This wouldn't be such a widespread problem if it weren't such a difficult thing to avoid. While drawing a gun out of a strong-side holster, you have some natural upward and forward momentum and body commitment that keep the gun heading to the target and usually prevent it from lasering your own body. Returning the gun to the holster, however, is a slower movement that requires you to crank your shoulder up into a chicken-wing position. This motion is uncomfortable enough for any of us, but large people and those with limited flexibility have a extra hard time doing it. We avoid this discomfort by raising our shoulders as little as possible. The less we raise our shoulders, the easier and more natural the reholstering stroke is, but the more we angle the gun's muzzle toward ourselves.

TWO SOLUTIONS

There are two reholstering techniques that solve this problem. The first is the right-angle reholstering stroke, which is the reverse of the right-angle draw stroke.

For years the standard draw stroke has involved the gun's muzzle moving in a straight line to the target as soon as it clears leather. With the right-angle draw stroke, you pull the gun straight up out of the holster until the base of your thumb is touching the side of your pectoral muscle, and then thrust the gun in a straight line to the target from there. This draw stroke has much to recommend it: you automatically clear any intermediate close-in obstacles such as a table (real life isn't like the range), you get the front sight into the cone of your vision sooner, a close-in assailant (which must be assumed, since it's the most likely case) will have a harder time jamming the draw and thus deflecting the gun's muzzle away from himself, as well as other benefits. (To see this method demonstrated in detail, I highly recommend that you view the *Jim Grover Defensive Shooting Series*, available from Paladin Press.)

For our purposes here, the key advantage of the right-angle reholstering stroke is that it's the exact reverse of the draw stroke. The gun comes straight back such that the base of the thumb makes contact with the side of the pectoral muscle. At this point, you simply point the gun south, ride your thumb down your ribs with the muzzle pointing directly downward, and reseat the gun into the holster. The key to

One safe way to reholster without "lasering" yourself is to bring the gun back to the outside side of the holster, then raise the gun until it "pops" over into the holster top opening.

making this technique work so you don't laser yourself is to keep the base of the thumb in contact with your ribs all the way down your side until the muzzle is in the holster.

The second safe reholstering technique is to bring the gun down comfortably to the outside of the holster and then ride the body-side of the gun up the holster until the muzzle jumps over into its top opening.

Both these techniques work and are "free" in the sense that we don't have to trade off or give up anything to obtain the benefits of their extra margin of safety. Free things are rare in this business. There's no reason not to incorporate one of them into our training and teaching. It's time that we stopped being hypocrites, stopped violating one of the cardinal safety rules that we all preach, and stopped needlessly endangering ourselves.

---

1. As responsible gun owners know, the four rules of firearms safety are: 1) Treat every gun as if it is loaded, 2) Never point a gun at anything you don't want to shoot, 3) Keep your finger off the trigger until you are ready to shoot, and 4) Be sure of your backstop.

CHAPTER 10

Extreme Close-Quarter Shooting

A Critical Examination of Close-In Shooting Techniques

HOUSTON, WE STILL HAVE A PROBLEM

Statistics indicate that most law enforcement officers are killed within 5 to 7 feet of their attackers. That's either at touching distance or within "one-step" distance. No one knows what the stats are for shootings not involving police officers, but all the educated bets are that the distances involved are even closer! Yet most firearms training does not begin to mirror this stark reality. Yes, it's encouraging to see that much more firearms training these days emphasizes 7- to 10-yard distances as opposed to the old 15- to 25-yard nonsense. But, at best, that's still three times too far away.

A curious thing happens

when we observe up-close shooting. Generally, shooting quickly and accurately under stress gets easier as we shorten up the distance. As we move from, say, 25 yards to 3 yards, the shooting becomes steadily easier. But as we move in from 3 yards, to 1 yard, and then right up to belly-to-belly distance, the shooting gets harder if we are at all cognizant of trying to ward off the opponent, not shoot ourselves, and keep our gun out of the opponent's disarm zone. After all, if you know how, it's pretty easy to disarm an attacker if you are within one step of him.

Now let's complicate the problem by assuming that you are shooting at an active assailant—that is, a person who suddenly assaults you from within 7 feet. Now your opponent will be on top of you before you can draw your gun, and both you and he (or they—the trend is for assaults by more than one assailant) will be moving rapidly. He may be much bigger than you. He may have a knife or club. Now things are much more difficult. Now you must obviously combine some sort of movement and empty-hand maneuver with the gun draw, and you must fire into your assailant in such a way that 1) he can't disarm you and 2) your gun doesn't jam.

Yes, I know that you should never get that close to a potential assailant. Well, let me say this about that to those who say so: Go back to your armchair and give me a *#@!%$& break!

Why don't we spend more time on this most likely shooting distance? Hell, why do many defensive shooters spend *no time at all* here? Well, here's how I see it:

- It goes against tradition. If long-range practice was good enough for Grandpa then it's good enough for us.
- It's difficult. This is the most difficult shooting to teach. The instructor may not know how to shoot effectively at this range. Moving from 7 yards to 1 yard is like moving from checkers to three-dimensional chess.

- It's dangerous. Shooting realistically at this range requires creative movement, and ranges are usually constrained to a single safe movement direction. Ranges can easily be made safe in almost 360 degrees of fire at these short distances by using tire stacks, but students can probably only fire one at a time in these spaces, which slows down the class. Few instructors bother with this.
- It requires knowledge of, and the integration of, both defensive tactics and firearms. It requires a true holistic use-of-force instructor to conduct this true use-of-force training. These people are rare.
- It's complicated. Why bother? I may be embarrassed.
- It hasn't become a subject with a well developed body of knowledge yet—there are only random techniques and anecdotes.

WHY ARE WE SHOOTING THIS GUY?

What we're talking about here is an attack in which you don't have time to immediately draw your gun—an attack in which you must use some empty-hand maneuver to redirect or stall the attack so that you can gain the time and possibly distance to draw and then shoot if necessary. But if you have just successfully used an empty-hand, nonlethal technique to avert the initial attack, why are you justified in then shooting this guy? Haven't you just demonstrated that lethal force isn't necessary?

Actually, no. While defensive training should emphasize many different resolutions to many different types of attacks at this close distance (including nonlethal force), there are many reasons why deadly force might still be necessary. Among them are the following:

- There is more than one attacker.
- The attacker is armed.

- There is a disparity in size, strength, and/or age between the defender and the assailant.
- The attacker is high on pain-killing drugs such as PCP, crack, or alcohol.
- The attacker has a history of violence.
- The attacker has specialized skills, such as martial arts training.
- The attacker is attempting to disarm the defender.

What matters is the totality of the circumstances. There is a difference between a little old grandmother shoving you over a parking space misunderstanding and a crack addict violently intent on killing you. Remember—it's the defender's reasonable perception of the threat at the time that counts. If you are reasonably in fear for your life and cannot escape, then shooting is justified.

An interesting argument is sometimes brought up in favor of shooting someone who knows you're armed and still directs an empty-hand assault at you. "If the defender loses that fist fight, he can then be disarmed and shot with his own weapon," it goes. That's certainly true, and many police departments teach their officers to shoot someone who is threatening them with OC (oleoresin capsicum) defense spray or Mace for just that reason. But if that's so, then why can't we shoot *anyone* who's getting physical with us and somehow knows we're armed? Well, again, it comes back to the defender's perception of the threat and the totality of the circumstances. That is, was a perception of immediate and unavoidable deadly or serious harm to the defender reasonable under the circumstances?

CAVEATS

There are some factors in an up-close assault that require a response specific to that particular kind of assault. The several approaches to the up-close attack problem that we discuss later are not necessarily suited to the following situations (although they may be, depending on the circumstances).

Knife attacks by anyone with even a modicum of skill should probably be met with an empty-hand-only response. The reason for this is that a knife attack is not strength- or power-dependent—a slight movement can severely injure you. Unlike with many other kinds of attack, deflecting or stalling a knife attack does not necessarily give you a reprieve. Empty-hand knife defense is a highly specialized, extremely difficult, widely misunderstood area. The shooting defenses discussed below may not be your best bet. (This subject is covered extensively in our video *Facing the Blade: Empty-Hand Against a Knife*.[1])

If the up-close attack is an attempt to take your gun, then regaining control of your weapon must be your first priority. If your up-close attack is by a gun-wielding person, then disarming him, not shooting him, may be the right response.

EVALUATING THE TECHNIQUES

So, given all that, what are the effective responses for shooting a person who is attacking you with deadly force within 7 feet? Let's examine the techniques commonly taught to solve the extreme close-quarters shooting (ECQS) problem. We'll look at the elements of the technique, discuss its pros and cons, and report the results of our acid test: actually trying it. (My God, what a concept!) The testing protocol was simple: we placed skilled shooters facing an opponent at a distance of 5 feet. The hands of both shooters were at their sides, and their guns were holstered in a speed scabbard. The attacker initiated an assault, and the defender was to draw and shoot the attacker using the technique under evaluation. The record of these trials is documented in my video *Extreme*

Close-Quarters Shooting: A Critical Analysis of Contact-Distance Shooting Tactics, available from Paladin Press.

Basically, very few of the standard techniques worked. In almost all cases a committed attacker is able to "kill" the defender before his gun even closely clears leather. This is further complicated by the basic rule of all physical encounters: size and strength count. A big attacker has all the advantages over a smaller defender. Life's not fair.

The Speed Rock

The Speed Rock is one of the oldest techniques taught for this purpose, dating, I believe, from the early 1900s. It is widely maligned—and widely misunderstood. It involves leaning back at the waist and firing your gun just as it clears your holster. It is very fast, and it has the virtue of denying the gun to your opponent. Opponents of this technique point out that it puts you severely off balance, and that's true. But the Speed Rock is intended only for those situations where there is no other alternative—when you are grabbed or pushed over something like the hood of a car. As Gabe Suarez says, "Keep the proper perspective on this technique. You are close enough to your enemy to smell the onions he had for lunch, [and] you *cannot* move back . . . " (From Suarez's excellent book, *The Tactical Advantage,* available through Paladin Press.)

Nevertheless, problems with the Speed Rock are that with so little clearance of the holster you can easily shoot yourself; it tends to shoot your opponent in the gut, which doesn't usually produce instant stops (remember, this guy's right on top of you); shooting at this contact distance can jam your slide; and it doesn't work if your back is up against the wall (you can't draw). This last objection is certainly valid for many techniques—it's hard to draw your gun when you're pinned against a wall no matter what technique you plan to implement—but applies particularly to the Speed Rock since it is touted as being suited for situations when you have no back room.

Finally, does it work? Our tests indicate it does not.

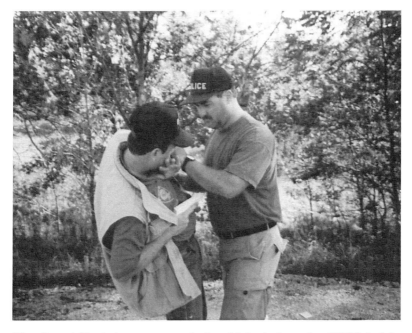

The Speed Rock is a commonly taught technique for ECQS but is fraught with logical and tactical errors.

Step Back/Shove 'n' Shoot

Probably the second most widely taught technique is to strike your opponent in the chest (usually with a palm-heel strike), take one or several steps back or to an angle, draw, and shoot. Many instructors advocate shooting while rapidly backpedaling several yards. This technique is instinctive, certainly, and is simple to teach dry-fire (but not live-fire—see below). However, a closer examination shows that it suffers from several faults in actual implementation, the most damning of which is that it requires defenders to move backward into an area they can't see. In many cases taking a single shuffle step backward or at an angle will not present a danger, since what's in that space is probably something the

The Step-Back technique is instinctive and widely taught—but dangerous. Try it full force someday in a cramped, crowded, littered apartment. Here knife instructor Mike DeBethencourt demonstrates what it looks like in theory.

defender is aware of. But taking many steps to any backward angle, particularly rapidly, is probably an invitation to disaster. The defender generally will have no idea what's there, and his visual perception will be hampered by the tunnel-vision effect of stress.

I've actually heard trainers tell me that this won't be a problem, since the defender just walked into this scene and will have noted what's now behind him as he entered! I'm not sure that this merits comment, except to note that it is apparently believed in some quarters. Even if defenders were focused on their surroundings to this extent—that is, were focused on the surroundings instead of the dangerous suspect (highly unlikely)—they probably won't remain in the same orientation to the escape route as when they entered the danger area, and even if they did remain so orientated, objects—other people, animals, etc.—may have moved in back of them.

Additionally, Mas Ayoob and others point out several flaws in the basic reasoning of this technique. Essentially, since you can't move backward as quickly as your attacker can move forward, you are depending on your strike to disable or disorient him long enough for you to draw. Think about this. As Mas says, "Have you ever struck someone with all your might and had no effect? Have you ever taken a solid blow yourself and not been affected? The answer is probably 'yes' to both questions. How then can we rely on a blow already weakened by our backward movement to stun an attacker who, by definition, is pumped up enough to kill or maim us?" Another assumption sometimes mentioned with this technique is that, if threatened with a gun, we become a smaller target by moving backward. Well, not in the time it takes the perp to pull a trigger we don't. Besides, I'm not too worried about being attacked on the nice, flat, open range. I worry about this happening in a narrow, junk-strewn alley, where there's not enough room to become a smaller target even if I could move fast enough.

Another point: For people who train in two-handed shooting the majority of the time, there is a trained "hand-meets-hand" reflex when shooting. Extending one hand to ward off an assailant while shooting with the other is likely to result in the defender's shooting his nonshooting hand. Also, if the defender extends his shooting arm he is presenting his gun to the perp or to someone else nearby for a potential disarm.

Finally, this technique just doesn't work against a committed attacker.

ANGLE FORWARD

A well thought-out response to the ECQS problem is the angle-forward technique taught by Marty Michelman of the Suffolk County, Massachusetts, Sheriff's Department. Here the defender uses both hands to deflect either the assailant's body or his arm while moving forward at an angle, thus winding up either in back of or to the side of the attacker. Then the defender draws the appropriate weapon—OC spray or gun, depending on the situation at that instant. (If you carry a gun, you *do* carry a flashlight, knife, and OC spray, don't you? If not, go sit in the corner.) This is an important feature of the Angle Forward technique—when it works, it provides the defender with the time and distance to draw an

The Angle Forward response to an extreme close-quarter attack is practical and is recommended.

appropriate weapon; it doesn't train the defender to always shoot when assaulted close in. This is an important training and liability issue, and this technique addresses the concern expressed earlier: *If you have just successfully used an empty-hand, nonlethal technique to avert an attack, why are you now justified in shooting this guy? Haven't you just demonstrated that lethal force is not necessary?*

Positive features of the Angle Forward technique are that when done correctly, it involves little strength and positions you at the offender's side or back. By moving forward, the defender is moving in a direction of his strength and to a visible, almost always open space (where the attacker just came from). Also, the defender is in no danger of shooting his hand.

Concerns about this technique are that it requires significant skill, and that it's not instinctive for many untrained people to move into an attack. Finally, this technique can work, but there must be a good amount of skill disparity between the defender and the attacker.

The Elbow Technique

This technique goes by several names, and variations of it are taught by several well-known instructors. Essentially, it involves dropping your center of gravity, taking a small step either forward or backward such that your gun side is to the rear, and raising your nonshooting elbow sharply upward into the attacker's neck or chest area while covering your head with your hand and forearm. Simultaneously, you draw to the pectoral retention position and shoot to the attacker's chest or pelvis.

This technique is very close to one's instinctive startle response of crouching and covering the head. It keeps the attacker somewhat away and thrusts a potentially powerful blow into a vulnerable area. The defender's balance remains solid, the gun stays back, and the draw happens under the assailant's line of vision. The defender's head and neck are

The Elbow technique is gaining popularity, but has its pros and cons.

protected, and the technique is not dependent on finding open space to move into.

Potential disadvantages to this technique are that, if done incorrectly, with the defender leaning too far forward, the back of his head and neck will be exposed and his balance broken. Also, because it involves some force against force, it may not work well for a small defender against a large opponent. One criticism leveled against this technique is that it can restrict your vision. This is true, but we must remember that a fight is dynamic—you don't stay frozen in one position while your opponent moves around you. Any technique that protects you—whether this Elbow technique, a boxer's slip, or whatever—restricts your vision momentarily but is often practical in the broader context of a rapidly changing situation.

Unfortunately, our tests showed that against a committed attacker, this technique usually falls apart.

Drive Forward

This technique will appeal to those with martial arts experience. Here, instead of deflecting the attack or moving back, you use your nonshooting arm to strike or drive into the opponent while simultaneously drawing your gun and shooting.

This technique adheres to the fundamental principles of conflict by employing what is always the most effective defense—a strong offense. It does not require the defender to move into unknown space, and it will probably greatly surprise the assailant, turning the "attacker's" advantage to the defender. Disadvantages are that it requires some strength, you have to be careful not to shoot your own hand or arm, the slide of your pistol may jam during a contact shot to your opponent, and it's not instinctive for most untrained people to move violently into their attacker. Also, if you meet resistance to your counteroffense, you can easily find yourself in a hand-to-hand fight instead of creating the time to draw your gun.

We found that the effectiveness of this technique was directly proportional to the unarmed skill level of the defender.

Drop to Deck

This technique involves dropping to the floor correctly—that is, onto your back by folding your leg and tucking your shin, keeping all four limbs off the ground, fighting from there if necessary, drawing, and shooting. This is a complicated technique, involving many difficult skills: falling correctly, keeping your limbs off the ground, and floor fighting. Once you're on the ground, you'll probably be there without other options until the conflict is over, which is pretty restrictive, and it's hard to fight on the floor and draw and

The Drive Forward—attacking the attacker—is one of the best responses available to you at close quarters. Here, even in this static pose, the intensity of South African instructor Henk Iverson is apparent. You'll need that kind of commitment and mind-set for this technique to work.

shoot all at once. Trained people can make this work, but it seems unlikely that the average person could learn it easily.

On the positive side, this is a great—nay, necessary—technique to have in your arsenal. If you fall or are pushed down, you're going to have to fight and shoot from the ground anyway, so you should know how to do it correctly. If there is no other escape route from a close-in assault, this may be your only option. From the floor you can often fire in all directions, and you may even gain the element of surprise for a fraction of a second by dropping like this.

The drop-to-the-ground technique is much more viable

There's a right way and lots of wrong ways to drop to the ground and fight. Here Henk Iverson demonstrates the right way. Note the intensity again.

than you might think. Our experience is that the first time it is done to him, each "attacker" just stands there with a blank "What the ****?" expression on his face. The key to making this technique work is to kick violently with a bicycling motion (NOT straight kicks) once you're on the ground, and then pull in your legs with ankles crossed and shoot when ready.

Certainly, however, being on the floor puts you at a considerable disadvantage in a multiple-assailant assault. This fact presents a logical difficulty: from it we might conclude that going to the floor is a better option against only one or two assailants, but then, without a whole bunch of assailants to block them, wouldn't there probably be other escape routes open?

Fight It Out

Basically, our tests showed that the sheer mechanics of an up-close (within 7 feet) attack make any attempt to draw a gun all but impossible. Given that a defender will have about a half-second reaction time, and then a draw time on top of that, and given the fact that an assailant can easily cover 7 feet inside of that time, we simply won't have time to draw and shoot. We are therefore advocates of integrated defense training. That is, it's not enough to just know the gun, you need to have empty-hand skills (and stick, knife, and OC spray skills) too. This is not just to make you a well-rounded person, but because the majority of attacks happen within this close distance where it's doubtful that you could bring your gun into play anyway.

I submit that we spend too much time trying to find gun solutions to inherently nongun problems, which statistics tell us describes most of the attacks we will face. Within 7 feet the correct—indeed probably the only, but certainly not the easy—answer to an assault is that our defense will require empty-hand skills. This is even more true when we realize that even if we manage to shoot our assailant at these distances before he kills us, he is probably going to continue to try to kill us for a while longer. People don't stop just because they're shot, and in this situation, they're right on top of us at the time.

Run!

Why not turn and run! This is really not a bad idea at all. If we're not police officers, we don't have a duty to intervene. What's wrong with turning tail and scooting? Why don't we include an exercise of turning and running as fast as we can to cover—say 15 yards away—and then drawing and shooting from there? It's not macho, but it's probably wise in many cases. It's not really a "shooting" solution, and it requires you to be in shape, but it's an option you'll want to have.

GENERAL PRINCIPLES

There are several general principles that emerge from thinking about the ECQS problem. No matter which technique you favor, these are:

- At less than 7 feet, speed wins, not skill.
- Attitude, smoothness, and control will probably determine who wins the encounter.

Discretion is the better part of valor. If you can run, do so! (Bruce Lee once called running a martial art.)

- People will naturally want to move their gun toward the threat, so any technique requiring shooting from a close-to-the-body position must incorporate locking the gun arm to the body.
- When designing techniques and exercises, always assume a 5-foot-tall, 100-pound defender against Mike Tyson on PCP.
- Make sure your technique will work in a crowded, cramped area. Anything will work on a nice, flat, open, controlled range.
- You usually want to move off the centerline of the attack.
- Assume multiple adversaries. Incorporate multiple targets and multiple lines of fire into your exercises.
- Use dummy guns to train on uneven terrain.
- Incorporate continual verbalization into your training: "Don't move," "Don't make me shoot you," etc.

Final Thought

Think about this: assuming that you understood the dynamics of the situation, if you were told before you got your gun that most attacks on you would happen within 7 feet, and you were offered the choice of intensive handgun training or intensive empty-hand training, which would you choose as a survival option?

Acknowledgments

Thanks to the many instructors who were kind enough to respond to my inquiries about this subject and educate me about it, particularly: Louis Awerbuck, Mas Ayoob, Mike Beckley, Bert DuVernay, John Farnam, Jim Grover, Phil Messina, Marty Michelman, Layne Schultetus, Dave Spaulding, and Gabe Suarez. I have borrowed many of their ideas in this chapter.

1. *Facing the Blade* by Ralph Mroz and Jeff Kunz is available for $39.95 plus $3.00 postage and handling from Defensive Research, P.O. Box 872, Greenfield, MA, 01302.

CHAPTER 11

Don't Forget the Little Things

It's easy to forget the details, the little things that can save your life. We get so focused on the gun, and maybe the holster, that we forget the other aspects of our dress and behavior that are important. We can get lured into regarding the gun as a talisman that will ward off evil.

The truth is that safety is a holistic discipline and, as with so many activities, success depends on attention to detail. Here are a few things to keep in mind.

BELTS

We don't want to draw attention to the fact that we're armed, both out of courtesy to the public and because it can get you killed in an encounter. Street predators have a pretty finely tuned sense of what makes a person dangerous to them, and they will spot the things that give your gun away, like one of those wide gun belts. In the '70s and early '80s, the only proper belts available that could bear the weight of a holstered handgun were those 1 3/4-inch-wide, fancy-stitched gun belts that are still popular. In those days, they could pass for a Western-style sport belt, but today they scream "gun" to those who know what they're looking for. (If you're inclined to wear a police duty-style Garrison belt, ditto, but in spades!) These days, there are a number of slim or slimmed-down belts designed specifically to support a gun, and they come in a variety of colors and styles—from sporty to Brooks Brothers. Jim Murnak/FIST makes some of the best. This is money very well spent.

SHOES

You might think that cautions about shoes apply only to vice cops stupid enough to wear their black duty shoes with plain clothes while trying to get solicited by hookers. But they apply to everyone. Whether you're armed or not, in a self-defense situation your feet will be moving fast—either to get you to cover or to fight. If you're wearing sandals, loafers, top-siders, or any other kind of shoe that comes off easily, you're going to lose them and impair your tactical ability—and probably trip ass over teakettle in the process. If you wear shoes with leather or another kind of slippery soles, you'll lose your footing when you need it most. High heels and platform shoes, it goes without saying, are pretty high up there on the stupid scale. Being prepared means that in addition to having a weapon and training you wear tie-up shoes with non-slip soles. Every time I buy a new pair of dress shoes, they go straight to the cobbler for rubber soles before I even wear them. Even if I'm not carrying a gun while wearing them, I may still get into an empty-hand self-defense encounter.

The running shoe on the right will tear, and the sole will rip off when subjected to lateral stress—which happens when you fight. You're better served by cross-trainers, such as the shoe on the left. Little things can make a big difference sometimes!

A note on athletic shoes. A lot of gun people wear running shoes with their jeans and gun. This is a bad practice. Shoes designed specifically for running are constructed with the outsole (the bottom sole) glued onto the shoe in such a way that it accommodates running only. These shoes do not allow for side-to-side or pushing-off type motions. If you use running shoes for activities requiring this type of motion—boxing, martial arts, etc.—you will sooner or later rip the outsole off the shoe. I've done just that on heavy bag workouts. Further, running shoes usually have very tacky outsoles, making it easy to trip when moving sideways. For casual wear, then, stick to cross-trainers, tennis shoes, or basketball shoes.

DRESS

Leave clothes with gun logos and slogans on them at home. A T-shirt that says "I have PMS and a gun—any questions?" is an offense to polite society, does wonders to raise funds for Handgun Control, Inc., and will get you executed first in a robbery. Likewise with that nifty golf shirt you picked up at the Smith & Wesson Academy. I like the guys at the academy a lot, but I don't wear their logo items in public.

COATS

If you're concealing a gun under a coat, for goodness sake, leave the coat unbuttoned! This is pretty straightforward, but you'd be amazed at the number of otherwise reasonably savvy people who commit this sin. Guns don't operate by telepathy—you have to access them!

OPULENCE

Food attracts insects, and money attracts human scum. Dress down, or at least conservatively and plainly. If you must gratify your ego by impressing someone with your material wealth, have the grace and good survival sense to do so in private. A good example of this is holster maker Jim Murnak, who lives in New York City. He doesn't carry his belongings in a briefcase, but rather in a plastic shopping bag. It's not elegant, but it doesn't attract muggers, either.

FLASHLIGHT

If you carry a gun, you must carry a flashlight. If you don't carry a gun, then you really have to carry a flashlight. If you're not a cop the flashlight isn't so much for tactical use in a low-light shooting situation or to search a structure with; it's meant to blind an opponent by shining it in his eyes, and

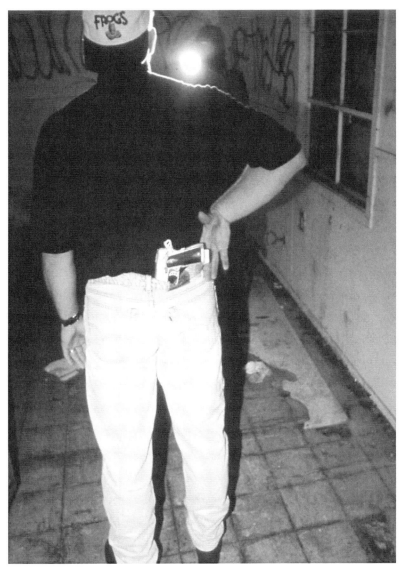

A strong white light is a necessity for self-defense. Most shootings occur in dim light, and a good light will blind your assailant. Photo courtesy of the *Sure-Fire Institute.*

it's used to scan potentially dangerous situations before entering them—such as approaching your car in a parking lot. There are some excellent small, bright lights out there, such as the Sure-Fire 6, 9, and 12 series. Don't buy a cheap light—lumens count here, and a small, ergonomic size means that you will really carry it. Don't leave home without one.

EYEGLASSES

It's only common sense that if you need corrective lenses to see, you'll need them to shoot and fight. That lesson was brought home tragically during the famous FBI Miami shoot-out, in which one agent lost his glasses early on in the fight and spent the time until he was killed looking for them. Count on losing your glasses during the first second of an encounter. If you need them to see or fight, then you'll just have to wear a retaining device (such as Croakies or Chums). That's not particularly elegant or always convenient, but really, what other choice do you have? To not do so is to fool yourself that you can survive.

Depending on whom you ask, either God or the devil is in the details. The point, either way, is that they count.

CHAPTER 12

Myths of Concealed Carry

More people than ever are carrying concealed firearms due, in large part, to the new "must issue" laws that have been passed by so many states.[1] The craft of concealed carry has come a long way from its early days; true concealment holster design dates back to the late 19th century but has really only come into its own in the last couple of decades. At the same time, full-power handguns in small, light packages have become numerous, particularly over the last few years. What all this means is that more and more people are now buying holsters designed to carry the tool to which they are entrusting their security.

Caveat emptor! There are a lot of myths and half-truths that have become part of "common knowledge." Relying on your range buddies or holster advertisements for practical advice is relying on the uninformed and the biased. Speaking as a cop, relying on the advice of cops is generally unsound, since so few of them are really into guns at all. Those who are into them usually are not thoughtful experts, but thank God there are enough exceptions. Besides, cops have badges, and if their off-duty pieces are spotted, there's no hassle (generally).

MYTHS

Myth No.1: The Small-of-the-Back (SOB) Holster Is an Ideal Concealed Carry Method

Actually, an SOB holster does a very good job of concealing your pistol, so long as you remain standing and don't bend over. Access from a standing position is quite good. But when you're sitting, the gun is inaccessible, very uncomfortable, and will cause back problems. Further, the gun is positioned directly over your lumbar disks, and there's many a person who has received a spinal injury from falling on his SOB-worn gun. Considering that your chances of falling are considerably greater than your chances of needing to use your gun for self-defense, this is a bad trade-off indeed!

Finally, during a struggle, it's much harder to draw your gun from an SOB position than from a strong-side hip position.

Myth No. 2: The Cross-Draw Holster Is Tactically Unsound

The cross-draw has its drawbacks, certainly. It's true that your arm can be pinned while drawing the gun with a simple press from your assailant. But if that's happening, then you're in a fight. You aren't going to just stand there and let him pin your arm—you're going to move. Indeed, you're already moving if you're that close to a person you think is a deadly threat. For anyone who's done any empty-hand training (as we all should) or integrated-use-of-force training, this is not the certain disaster that so many writers would have us believe. This "fatal drawback" is really just an excellent example of armchair analysis.

The cross-draw is really the only practical way to carry a gun for someone who spends a lot of time driving or in a car. Any other position is either uncomfortable and/or eventually causes back problems—not to mention that gun access is slow or denied.

But beware! Many holster manufacturers make "driving" holsters, which are cross-draw rigs that snap on and off. The idea is that you keep the rig in your car, snap it on when you enter, remove your gun from its normal carry position (usually the strong-side hip), and slip it into the driving holster. When you exit the car, the reverse procedure is followed. HUH??? If I'm going to drive for eight hours straight this might work, but what if I'm running errands all over town? The most fatal flaw is that if I have to exit my vehicle in a hurry (say I'm being ambushed), these driving holsters don't hold the gun all that securely, and I'll lose it. So just when I need my gun the most, these holsters are designed to lose it for me!

Myth No. 3: The Inside-the-Waistband (IWB) Holster Is More Concealable Than an Outside-the-Pants Holster

Obviously, this is technically true. But not by much. A normal gun extends a couple inches below the belt line in a pancake holster—that's the difference here, a couple of inches. If the garment you wear to conceal your holster-carried gun is so short that you feel the necessity to gain a couple inches with an IWB, then the garment is probably too short to begin with. Sitting, reaching, and other movements will cause the garment to ride up much more than that in the course of a day's events. And yes, it's true that a well-made IWB will generally pull the gun in tighter to your body than a well-made outside-the-pants holster. But if we're talking about well-made holsters from the top makers, the difference is very small. Choose a top-quality holster and a properly fitting garment that's long enough to begin with, and both problems disappear.

Myth No. 4: Deep Concealment Is a Really Nifty Way to Carry Your Gun

Once we look at the definition of "deep concealment," this myth becomes obvious. "Deep concealment" means a position that's invisible but difficult to access, and since fast access is the primary rule in weapon tactics, deep concealment is obviously at odds with the very reason we carry a gun. Attacks happen at your attacker's initiation and at his convenience. And they happen fast! You usually will not have warning enough to have the gun in your hand when the attack goes down (which is yet another reason to integrate empty-hands skills with firearms skills). Your draw time is crucial, while your marksmanship at typical assault distances is not an issue. Fractions of a second can count. In general, you want to be able to draw and fire your weapon in 1 1/2 seconds from wherever you carry it. Systems that require you to dig a gun out of your pants leg or underwear don't make this grade. Further, most deep concealment systems require the use of two hands to access the gun, eliminating your empty-hand defenses.

To be fair, though, sometimes it's deep concealment or no gun. We all have those days and those circumstances. Just don't be under any illusions about the compromises you make.

Myth No. 5: The Ankle Holster Is Tactically Sound

An ankle-holstered gun is awfully close to deep concealment, so the comments above pretty much apply; they warrant separate mention because they're so common. It's true that with training you can access an ankle-carried gun in not much more time than you can a hip-carried gun. But citing this fact as a validation of the soundness of the ankle rig is another example of armchair analysis. Get out of that

The ankle holster's fatal disadvantage is shown here. It requires you to be stationary and off balance as you draw. There's no way to get to that gun in time in a typical spontaneous real-life attack.

Barcalounger, run through some realistic scenarios, and see what happens.

Whichever technique you use to draw from an ankle holster, you must remain stationary and bend over. You can't put distance or obstacles between you and your adversary, and you must assume a vulnerable position. Within 25 feet or so, your attacker will be on top of you before you clear leather (and most attacks happen within 5 feet). The only time in my life that I needed to draw a gun from an ankle holster, I was in just this impossible position. Fortunately, we all survived—but I've never carried there again! This experience so affected me that I don't even consider the ankle a good place for a back-up gun anymore. To me, an ankle holster is deep concealment—a way to carry a gun if the only alternative is to go unarmed.

Myth No. 6: "Fruit of the Loom" Holsters Are Really OK

You know what I'm talking about—those flimsy suede or nylon clip-held IWB holsters that you pick up for $10. They're a real bargain—Not! Go figure—someone spends hundreds of dollars on a good gun, to which he entrusts his life (which is worth at least a few bucks), and probably buys some books, videos, or in-person training, and then skimps on the thing that enables that life-saving tool to be carried reliably and comfortably.

Gun writers have forever preached the risks in these kinds of holsters, and they are right. They do not hold the gun securely to your body, you can't reholster the gun with one hand, and the gun falls out of them easily. The clips on them tend to not hold well, with the result that either the holstered gun pops off your belt or you draw a holstered gun with the trigger port blocked—a potentially fatal event. This has happened to me, fortunately during practice.

Now, these holsters, particularly the "better" models with recurved clips, do have their place. When carrying a gun off-body (in a briefcase, backpack, etc.), I slip one of these holsters into the case with the gun. Their flimsiness allows them to compress and not take up space, yet I have a ready way to slip the gun into my waistband should I need or want to. I just realize their limitations in that situation.

Myth No. 7: You Can't Conceal a Big Gun

Sure you can. You just have to use an appropriate holster, belt, and concealing garment. I'm thin at 6 feet tall, but when it was my duty gun, I used to comfortably conceal a 4-inch L-frame S&W 686 .357 Magnum under a sport coat. It was no big deal. And I know people both smaller and lighter than myself who regularly conceal similar-sized guns.

Actually, the correlation between size and concealability isn't all that linear. There are a lot of variables in the gun's profile and size, and the wearer's body type has a lot to do with it. My Kel-Tec is about as concealable and comfortable to carry as my Glock 19, yet the S&W 2-inch snubbie, which is similar in size to the Kel-Tec, is better in each department.

In fact, size affects comfort more than concealability, and experience will have to tell you what works for you. One area that's not much mentioned in this regard is the way you carry yourself. As Mas Ayoob has said, "When you first start to carry a gun, you feel like a person strapped to a gigantic gun. But after a while, it just goes away." True, and part of the reason is that you learn how to walk, bend over, etc. in such a way that the gun isn't exposed. Learning this skill is really far more important, concealment-wise, than the size of the gun you carry.

Myth No. 8: The Belt-Slide Holster Is a Mark of a Professional

The belt-slide holster is a sawed-off, semi-formless, bikini-like abbreviated pancake holster. An awful lot of the professional teachers who write for popular magazines appear in their photographs wearing one. I don't know why. Maybe it's because the slide of the gun is exposed and they think it looks cool. Maybe because it's a fast holster to draw from.

But they are not tactically sound. They work fine on the range, where all they have to do is hold a gun onto your belt, but in a realistic defensive situation, they are a considerable liability. Being generally unmolded and with no retention strap, they do not hold the gun securely. Sawed off (i.e., not extending much below the belt line), the slide is easily punched up and the gun pushed out of the holster by an upward movement of your thigh—or merely by your sitting down.

These are good holsters for the range, accommodating several guns of the same general shape or of the same family. But they are not seen among the REAL professionals who go and do. They are fine for practicing El Presidente on a flat, sunny range, but they are not found on folks practicing the more realistic exercise of bailing out of a car and squirming around on the ground to reach cover and shoot.

Myth No. 9: Shoulder Holsters Are Impractical

Shoulder holsters are really nothing more than uncomfortable cross-draw holsters, and all the earlier comments about them apply. They have one unequaled place in concealed carry, though. Under a buttoned up winter coat, they provide the only way to quickly access your gun.

Myth No. 10: The Holster
Is of Secondary Importance to the Gun

Actually, as I've said many times, the holster is more important than the gun. It's hard to buy a gun that's not reliable and accurate at defensive distances from a major manufacturer these days. But it's all too easy to buy a sloppy, ill-fitting, unconcealable, or dangerous holster. The holster system (holster, belt, and concealing garments) are what ensure that you'll actually have your defensive tool at hand when you need it. If they do not provide comfortable carry, you won't carry your gun at all. If it does not ride stably on you, it will be uncomfortable, access will be compromised, and concealment will be affected. If it does not provide a secure fit, you may lose your gun.

The rule is: Buy the most potent gun that's comfortable for you to shoot, and then invest whatever you need to acquire a top-shelf holster system to carry it.

Myth No. 11: Off-Body Carry
Is Not Worthy of Consideration

Off-body carry—in a purse, briefcase, ruck, etc.—is often maligned as ignorant or stupid. Folks who say this point out that your gun's access speed is considerably delayed, your

Off-body carry has a lot going against it, but sometimes it's all that's possible. If it's the only way you can carry, you must simply recognize the constraints you're under.

gun conveyance can be taken from you, and it is difficult to get to the gun while doing all the other moving and fighting that you'll have to do when under attack.

That's all absolutely true.

But for many of us some of the time, the alternative to off-body carry is to go completely unarmed. Certainly being armed is better. What *is* stupid, though, is to carry off body and to not realize the limitations inherent in that mode. And what's *really* stupid is to carry off body and not practice drawing from there.

CONCLUSION

There are reasons that most professionals carry their gun in a strong-side hip holster whenever they can. That is the most natural and fastest place to draw a gun from conceal-ment, it provides excellent concealment, and you can draw from that position while fighting. It's not new or noteworthy, but it works!

1. About 30 states now have laws stipulating that the state must issue a firearms permit to an applicant unless there is a compelling reason—usually a criminal record—not to. This is in contrast to the previous situation in many of these states where permits were either unavailable or issued arbitrarily.

CHAPTER 13

Thoughts on Ready Positions

by Bert DuVernay

This chapter and the following one are by Bert DuVernay, the director of the prestigious Smith & Wesson Academy. In addition to Bert's place at the helm of one of the world's leading firearms schools, Bert is a former police sergeant and is one of the most respected authorities in the firearms training world. He is also one of the finest thinkers and analysts in the business.

Ready positions for either the handgun or shoulder arm are basic to the proper use of the gun but don't seem to have benefited from much thought. For example, far too many people use the method of holding the muzzle beside the head, and we now see the chest-high ready position being taught by those that are heavily influenced by IPSC and similar competition. The first example seems to be nothing more than the figment of some movie director's imagination, and the second makes muzzle control in a dynamic environment impossible.

Let's look at what we expect a ready position to accomplish for the responsible defensive shooter. First, the ready position should be a technique that consists of as much of our shooting position as possible, or at least prepares the body to assume the shooting position rapidly and consistently. Since, as Cooper says, the object of shooting is hitting, and since the defensive shooter must hit quickly, the relationship between the ready position and the fundamentals of stance and grip is evident.

Second, although of equal if not greater importance than the first, the ready position must lend itself to good muzzle control. It must permit the practical shooter to move without crossing others, particularly nonhostiles, with the muzzle. Muzzle control is a fundamental safety issue. It cannot be disregarded because it is inconvenient. I have heard instructors, some of whom I have great respect for, say that if the shooter has been properly trained to keep the finger out of the trigger guard until the shot is begun, muzzle control in a dynamic environment is unnecessary. That seems to be a questionable position. Many of our students have told me that they commonly observe breaches of trigger-finger discipline during stressful simulation or role-play training. Many of these breaches were committed by officers considered to be highly disciplined at keeping the finger outside the trigger guard.

Lt. Dave Spaulding, Montgomery County, Ohio, sheriff's office, believes that under stress the shooter subconsciously confirms the position of the trigger. Out of 674 officers that he observed during FATS training, 632 of them periodically placed their fingers in the trigger guard. This number includes many highly skilled and motivated officers, including graduates of S&W Academy, Gunsite, and Lethal Force

Institute. The officers that he has observed doing these "trigger searches" had no memory of doing so. If an officer was startled or bumped during a trigger search the results would be predictable. Thus, it is obviously not safe to disregard the issue of muzzle control. We cannot use the excuse "we are professionals" to justify the disregard of fundamental safety issues when they are inconvenient. We achieve "professional" standing only when we can obey our most basic safety rules even when they are inconvenient.

Muzzle control also involves not endangering ourselves with the muzzle. Letting the handgun "dangle" at the side usually involves crossing various parts of our anatomy with the muzzle. Bringing the gun up beside the head in TV fashion puts the muzzle far too close to the head for comfort in the event of a discharge, even if the bullet passes the head without contact.

Third, the ready position must not be so fatiguing that we cannot use it to cover a suspect until help arrives. In some areas the wait for help can be a very long one. Even in urban areas, if communications are interrupted, one might have to hold someone at gunpoint for longer than just a few minutes. When this happens, things are bad enough without having to invent a new covering technique at the same time.

Since movement is a tactical necessity, there is a fourth factor. The ready position must permit movement without compromising whatever advantage the shooter might have. The gun should not precede the shooter when entering an uninspected area, lest the shooter be disarmed. The ready position should be flexible enough to permit the muzzle not to lead the shooter into a room, but with minimal impact on the ability to place a shot quickly and accurately.

Related to movement, there is the issue of protecting the firearm from physical attack. Although I have serious reservations about teaching people to shoot from so-called hip positions, there remains a need to protect the gun from close

Bert DuVernay demonstrates a commonly taught ready position. This is a good one but has some drawbacks.

This version of the previous ready position corrects many deficiencies.

The chest-high ready position is favored by many CQB teams, although there are some safety trade-offs.

This modified version of the chest-high ready position helps prevent covering your teammates with your muzzle.

physical attack, and the ready position should lend itself to that concern. As with many things, if our firearms techniques are consistent with our other defensive skills, life is much simpler and safer.

Another consideration comes to us from the case of *George Washington and Darryl Hicks v. Skystone Lambert and City of Santa Monica* [1996 U.S. App. Lexis 27860, Case No. 94-56685, Oct. 28, 1996, 9th Circuit]. In this case the court specifically mentioned that whether or not police point their guns directly at the subject of an investigatory stop is a factor in deciding when the stop becomes an arrest. This particular case resulted in the officer's losing his qualified immunity and being held personally liable for a $20,000 judgment and $100,000 to $300,000 in fees and costs.

There may be other concerns as well, but I believe that these are the most important criteria to use to judge a ready position. In addition, the shooting technique utilized also affects the choice of ready position. Some positions seem to work well for a Weaver shooter but not for an isosceles shooter or vice versa.

Now that we have a framework for evaluation, let's examine a few common ready positions.

One common option is to just allow the shooting position to pivot down from the shoulders, keeping the elbows and wrists as they were in the shooting position. This position is very simple and quick to master. The shooting position is assumed quickly by simply pivoting the arms up to the line of the target. Muzzle control is extremely good with this position since the gun can be moved to either side readily. When you are operating in a team environment, this position has the added benefit of making it difficult for a person who is immediately in front of you to suddenly move in front of your muzzle. If your ready position "overlaps" your teammate's torso, a movement toward your gun will push your arms and gun aside.

The arms are lowered until they make contact with the torso in this ready position. This allows the gun to be kept at ready for long periods without excessive fatigue, but with the isosceles position the muzzle can be very close to the feet. Safe movement is easily accomplished by again diverting the muzzle toward one side or the other. This position is probably at its weakest in the handgun retention aspect, although it can be rapidly withdrawn to a position close to the hip for protection. Once that is done, though, it really becomes a different ready position. This technique can also be applied to the long gun by leaving the stock mounted and depressing the muzzle.

The chest-high (level with the pectoral muscles) ready position involves having the muzzle forward and the elbows spread apart and drawn back until the wrists or forearms touch the chest. This position has become popular with some special operations groups and is taught as an option by Bob Taubert (former FBI Hostage Rescue Team) in our CQB pistol class. It is very fast for an isosceles shooter but does not lend itself to the Weaver position. It is easy to maintain for long periods of time. The gun is close to the body for protection, but muzzle control during movement (or the movement of others) is impossible. I have not seen anyone using this position control the muzzle adequately. Practitioners of this technique usually offer the explanation that since muzzle control in a dynamic environment is impossible to achieve anyway, it should be disregarded. I don't believe that this position will be defensible, either morally or legally, when an officer or citizen is shot unintentionally.

As Taubert explains, the problem with the chest-high ready position can be remedied with a slight modification to the technique. If that position is assumed and then the forearms are depressed to a level between the ribcage and the beltline, there is now enough wrist flexion to permit very good muzzle control during movement or to avoid moving

The "Sabrina" position referred to in the text (technically, this is the "Low Sabrina"). This position actually has much to recommend it and is used by some very real folks.

The "High Sabrina" is a Hollywood invention and serves only to keep the gun in the same camera shot as the actor's face. DuVernay has a hard time suppressing a smirk as he demonstrates.

persons. It is not quite as good as the first ready position discussed, but it is certainly good enough to use in a practical environment. This technique may be a trifle slower to shoot from than the higher position, but not enough to be evident without a PACT timer. Once one considers the uncertainty of "stopping power" on the street, it is certainly not so much slower as to affect the outcome of a fight. The other aspects of the technique remain about the same. Neither of these variations has any application to the long gun.

The third ready position is normally not taken too seriously and consists of the muzzle being raised so that the front sight is at about the eyeline and the elbows are bent. I have heard this derisively referred to as the "Sabrina" position (as in Kate Jackson's character on *Charlie's Angels*) due to its popularity on television. I did not take this position seriously until seeing the defensive tactics techniques that are available from this position as taught by Duane Dieter. Dieter teaches a very strong muzzle-up ready position with the gun held away from the face, but with a bend in the elbows. Since this is not a chapter on defensive tactics, it is sufficient to say at this point that the techniques are very effective but should be reserved for serious threats. It is easy to defend the gun in this position using Dieter's techniques.

Muzzle control during movement is good and permits an alternative to a problem too seldom considered. The muzzle-down techniques that seem so safe on the range take on a different character inside a multistory structure with wood floors. Persons on the next floor down could easily be endangered by an unintended shot through the floor. Of course, people on the floor above are endangered by the Sabrina technique, but at least it provides an option for the trainer to consider. The fatigue factor is a serious one with this technique because if the elbows drop and the sight is kept on the eyeline, the muzzle comes closer to the face, resulting in an unsafe condition. The technique seems to work equally well with either Weaver or isosceles positions. It also works for long guns if the gun is held in such a way that it projects from the body. If the muzzle drifts back toward a "port arms" type position, the shooting platform is totally lost and ceases to be what I consider a ready position. It is very fatiguing with the long gun.

This last technique also provides a partial solution to the problem of muzzle control when searching with weapon-mounted lights. As normally taught, if the shooter is illuminating a suspect the muzzle is on that person whether shooting has started or not. This is a clear violation of safety rule 2, and some agencies have not mounted lights, on their shoulder arms in particular, because of this problem. When one considers that the ceilings and walls of most residential and office buildings are either white or lightly colored, the powerful lights (i.e., Laser Products) found mounted on most shoulder arms will illuminate the area sufficiently when pointed at the ceiling, avoiding the need to cover a storekeeper or homeowner with a muzzle while determining identity. I label this only a partial solution to the problem since it would be of limited utility in a warehouse and of no use at all outdoors.

As with many things, sometimes we do or teach something so long that it seems the only legitimate way to do things. The techniques taught by Bob Taubert and Duane Dieter have caused me to reevaluate such a simple thing as the ready position, and I'm glad they did.

CHAPTER 14

Street Safety
by Bert DuVernay

The whole purpose of what we do as firearms/use-of-force instructors is to make our students safer. That purpose becomes especially clear when you see a police agency refer to the firearms and defensive tactics instructors as the Occupational Safety Unit, as in the case of the South Australia Police. All too often, though, we see safety treated as something to consider on the range with too little concern about how the same issues would be treated on the street.

One example that comes to mind is the concept of "downrange." We relentlessly preach that the muzzle should be pointed in no other direction than downrange. While that is generally a safe procedure, it should be realized that it does not prepare our students for the safe use of firearms *off* the range. Once the student is removed from the static, sterile, square range environment, he or she finds that there is no reference point for the muzzle. At that point, downrange becomes the area to the front of the student, no matter which way he or she is facing and no matter what is in front of the student. The bottom line is that we have substituted the very limited concept of downrange for the far more useful concept of muzzle control.

This explains why our students cover each other with their muzzles so much on the street. The concept of downrange is largely a crutch for muzzle control that we kick out from beneath our students when they leave the range. If we want people to control their muzzles in a dynamic environment we must teach them specifically how to do that.

Rule 2 (of the four safety rules) tells us that we must not allow our muzzles to cross anything that we are not willing to put a hole in. People who use firearms in public must learn to be constantly aware of their muzzle projection (the potential bullet path) and their surroundings. Once aware of those two things, they must not permit that muzzle projection to cross anything that they can't live with shooting. This must be subconscious behavior if a person is to be truly safe with a firearm in public, or even in a home-defense situation. If it is only done when consciously addressed, it won't happen under stress when the mind is concerned with other matters.

In order for that level of muzzle control to be displayed, we must give students experience at handling firearms under other circumstances than on that square, static, sterile training range mentioned previously. The first step is training in pivots and turns. Once the student learns how easy it is to move the muzzle from one point to another without crossing others, the stage is set to progress. Exercises with Simunitions are good tools for the development of muzzle control if students are critiqued accordingly. One-piece training guns can also be used to safely conduct exercises that lend themselves to the critique of muzzle control. That critique is the key. If students don't have correct and incorrect gun handling practices pointed out, they can't improve their technique.

A related issue is the draw from shoulder holsters, waist packs, and the like. Students using these items are often placed on the far left end of the line (assuming they are right-handed) or prohibited from using those items on the range at all because they are "unsafe." If they are unsafe on the range, how can they possibly be safe in a crowded restaurant or in a K-Mart parking lot? While I have no problem with putting students using that type of equipment on the end of the line until they become known to the instructor, they shouldn't be permitted to use that equipment on the street until the instructor would be confident having them at any point in the line. There is a safe technique for drawing from those holsters, and until it is mastered, that person should not be permitted to use the equipment in public. If a person was unintentionally injured through the poor use of that equipment and it became known in court (and it would!) that you would not permit such equipment on the range because it was unsafe, how could you possibly put it in perspective? If it isn't safe on the range, it isn't safe on the street.

Trigger-finger discipline is another issue. It is well known that premature placement of the finger within the trigger guard too often results in the premature discharge of the weapon, sometimes with tragic results. However, we still occasionally see drills that place such an emphasis on delivering a fast shot that the only way students can "pass" is to place their fingers on the triggers at the ready position. What we condition students to do on the range, they will take with them to the street.

Frankly, I'm not sure what such drills are supposed to accomplish in the first place. While they may be of great value for a shooter entering competition, they have little relevance to the street. The International Wound Ballistics

Association has documented that it takes at least several seconds to force incapacitation on a determined attacker with cardiovascular hits. Viewed in that light, trying to shave hundredths of a second off a shot time at the expense of safety seems foolish.

Further, these drills seem to condition the shooter to quickly shoot at the first hint of visual or audible stimulation, without any thought. When would that be a useful skill on the street? I know of at least one bad shooting in which this seems to have been a primary factor. An officer had just returned from a course that emphasized this type of drill. During a building entry the officer shot the occupant, who, he later realized, had not posed any danger or given the officer any reason to be threatened. Fortunately the person was not seriously hurt (which gives me further reason to doubt the effectiveness of this type of training). It seems to me that this type of training breeds the bad habit of prematurely entering the trigger guard at the same time that it teaches shooting without the perception of a deadly threat. This is a real street safety problem from two perspectives.

Another practical safety issue that goes unaddressed is the one of misses. This relates to the issue of backstops and the downrange concept. When a student misses on the range there is a tendency to disregard the issue except for the failure to gain any points with that shot. It is as if the errant bullet somehow vanishes once it passes the target. This viewpoint is obtained through the presence of the backstop that is downrange. This viewpoint seems to be particularly prevalent when using buckshot. Rule 4 states that we must always be sure of our target and its background. This makes a great deal of sense on the range or while hunting, but how does it translate into action during a fight? Does it mean that we can't shoot unless there is a windowless brick wall behind our attacker? Of course not. It means that we must strike the torso of our attacker with every bullet we launch.

There are no misses on the street. There are only unintended targets. Every bullet we launch hits something. Critiques of a student's performance during simulation exercises should include this issue. Naturally, if we are trying to improve a student's long-distance shooting skill there will be misses. The problem arises when students do not progress past the point of static basic skills training and are left with the impression that misses don't matter as long as they get a few hits. I feel that this is a major contributing factor to the spray-and-pray approach to threat resolution. Too often, students leave the range feeling that they can get hits if they launch a sufficiently high number of shots.

One simple way to resolve this training issue might be to set up a simple scenario after the basic marksmanship practice has ended. In this scenario the shooter must only shoot when he is certain of a hit and hold his fire and withdraw or advance using cover when beyond the range of a certain hit. Students must make their own decisions about when to shoot since that is exactly what they must do on the street. The shooting decision involves not only the actions of the attacker but the students' self-assessment of ability under that circumstance. Students can be trained to make this portion of the shooting decision even before they are exposed to what we normally think of as scenario-based training.

The lack of proper holster skills is also a major safety issue. People who are not confident of their ability to hit quickly from the holster tend to get the gun out prematurely. This tendency compounds the muzzle control and trigger finger discipline issues discussed earlier. If students cannot promptly get the gun back in the holster with one hand and without looking, they tend to leave it in their hands, or worse, when they no longer need it. I possess a videotape that shows an officer placing his handgun on the sidewalk within arm's reach of a downed, but very animate suspect shot by other officers. The officer in question needed his portable radio but found that his hands were occupied, one with his handgun. The officer clearly had no confidence in his ability to holster his gun smoothly or had never been trained to do so. In any event, this lack of holster skill could have very easily caused the situation to escalate.

With the exception of some Browning design clones, all the guns that we would consider carrying for defense are designed in such a way that the firing pins cannot go forward unless the trigger is held to the rear. Any holster to be considered for defense use should cover the trigger guard. Taken together, these two design features assure that a gun in a holster is not going to fire. This is a major safety consideration. When the gun is no longer needed, put it away. This seems obvious, but if that "putting away" skill isn't well developed, the gun will stay in the hand under stress. This has the probability of being a real danger in a situation that first seemed to require the gun but winds up as a physical control problem.

The realization of practical firearms safety is a matter of training. Some of that training could be called safety training, but much of it is incorporated in other topical areas. It is too easy to look at safety as being for the other guy or as a topic that is so elementary that it is below us. The reason that we arm ourselves in the first place is to provide for our safety. To use our weapons in an unsafe manner defeats the purpose.